big
one-star
quilts
by magic

- Diamond-Free® Stars from Squares & Rectangles

- 14 Stars in 4 Sizes, 28 Quilting Designs, 4 Projects

Nancy Johnson-Srebro

C&T PUBLISHING

Text copyright © 2008 by Silver Star, Inc.

Artwork copyright © 2008 by C&T Publishing, Inc.

Quilting designs copyright © 2008 by Veronica Nurmi

Publisher: Amy Marson

Creative Director: Gailen Runge

Acquisitions Editor: Jan Grigsby

Editor: Liz Aneloski

Technical Editors: Ellen Pahl and Joyce Lytle

Copyeditor/Proofreader: Wordfirm Inc.

Cover & Book Designer: Christina D. Jarumay

Production Coordinators: Kirstie L. Pettersen and Casey Dukes

Illustrator: Kirstie L. Pettersen

Photography by Luke Mulks and Diane Pedersen of
C&T Publishing, unless otherwise noted

Published by C&T Publishing, Inc., P.O. Box 1456, Lafayette,
CA 94549

IMPORTANT LEGAL NOTICE:

The methods and techniques shown in this book for
making Eight-Point Star designs have been issued U.S.
Patent No. 7,194,970 and are fully protected by U.S. and
international copyright laws against unauthorized use
and infringement.

Library of Congress Cataloging-in-Publication Data

Johnson-Srebro, Nancy.

  Big one-star quilts by magic : diamond-free stars from squares & rect-
angles--14 star blocks in 4 sizes, 28 quilting designs, 4 projects / Nancy
Johnson-Srebro.

    p. cm.

  Summary: "Instructions for making 14 star blocks in 4 sizes using Nancy's
patented method for Diamond-Free® stars from squares and rectangles.
Includes 4 projects and 28 quilting designs"--Provided by publisher.

  ISBN 978-1-57120-461-5 (paper trade : alk. paper)

  1. Patchwork--Patterns. 2. Quilting--Patterns. 3. Patchwork quilts. 4.
Stars in art. I. Title.

  TT835.J58583 2008

  746.46'041--dc22

                                      2008003219

Printed in China

10 9 8 7 6 5 4 3

dedication

Over twenty years ago I started a trek in the quilting world, and since then I have met many, many wonderful people. Some of them became good friends, and I must say I've enjoyed memorable times with almost everyone. Without you, I wouldn't still be writing books.

With this in mind, I dedicate this latest book to all quilters who have had an impact on my life.

acknowledgments

To my quilt team: Karen Bolesta, Karen Brown, Molly Culp, Debbie Donowski, Heidi Escobar, Wendy Hopkinson, Nancy Jones, Beth Anne Lowrie, Janet McCarroll, Vicki Novajosky, Ellen Pahl, Pam Quentin, Laura Reidenbach, Marcia Rickansrud, and Rocky Sidorek. I couldn't do it without your support and help.

Special thanks to quilter Veronica Nurmi. Your incredible quilting design skills and talents continue to amaze me.

A big thank-you to the entire C&T staff, especially my longtime editors, Liz Aneloski and Ellen Pahl. You are not only my editors—we've also become good friends!

I offer a sincere thank-you to the following companies. Your fine products make quiltmaking easy.

American & Efird
Bernina of America, Inc.
Fairfield Processing Corporation
FreeSpirit
Hobbs Bonded Fibers
P&B Textiles
Prym Consumer USA, Inc.
RJR Fabrics
Robert Kaufman Co., Inc.
Superior Threads
The Warm Company

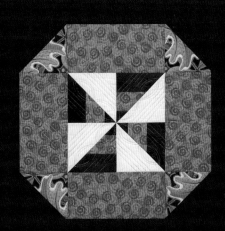

contents

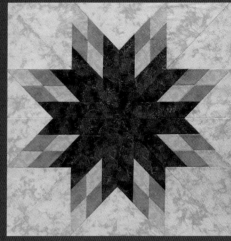

INTRODUCTION

After *Stars by Magic* was published,
introducing my Diamond-Free method,
we were inundated with requests for
instructions on how to make even
larger stars using this method.

Well, here they are! Everything you
asked for is included: 14 different stars
in 4 different sizes, ranging from large
wallhanging to king-size; 14 patterns
for incredible bonus wallhangings
using the cut-offs; 28 quilting designs;
4 Quilt Maps, for easy quilt assembly;
and, last but not least, 4 ways to make
bonus backings. All this from *squares
and rectangles!*

Enjoy and just remember . . . I warned
you that the methods presented in this
book are addictive!

Nancy

the basics

quilting basics

fabric and thread choices

If you're going to put time and energy into making quilts, use good-quality 100% cotton fabrics. This will help ensure that your quilts will be around for generations of family members to enjoy. If possible, prewash the fabrics before using them. This ensures that the fabrics are preshrunk and the dyes won't bleed if your block or quilt must be washed in the future.

All my machine piecing is done with Mettler 100% cotton, silk-finish thread, 50/3 weight. For most of my piecing, I use a light beige thread (color #703 or #810).

Various types and colors of Superior threads were used to machine quilt all the bonus quilts and the four quilts in the Quilt Map section.

 Easy on the Eyes!

Use navy blue thread on black fabric and black thread on navy blue fabric, so you can easily see the thread if you need to rip out a seam.

rotary cutting equipment

Use accurately printed rulers, such as Omnigrid or Omnigrip products. I found the Diamond-Free 6″ × 14″ and 8½″ × 24″ and the 20½″ square Omnigrip rulers to be most helpful when cutting out the big stars. Also, the 4″ × 36″ OmniEdge ruler is invaluable for drawing long diagonal lines on the Unit 2 pieces.

I prefer the Omnigrid mat because it's reversible—green on one side and light gray on the other side. I use the light gray side of the mat for cutting because the color contrasts more sharply with medium and dark fabrics.

Be sure to use a rotary cutter that is suited to your personal style and physical needs. I've found that either the Dritz

45mm or Omnigrid 45mm pressure-sensitive rotary cutter allows me to rotary cut for hours without hand fatigue.

 my favorite things

If your ruler slips while rotary cutting, place a sheet of Invisigrip on the back of the ruler. This product will prevent your ruler from slipping. It also works great on the back of templates!

no-fail rotary cutting

There are only two shapes used throughout the Big Star patterns in this book: a square and a rectangle. Both are very easy to rotary cut.

The cutting chart for each block gives the cut measurements of the squares and rectangles. This will determine the width of the strip you will cut. For example, if the instructions require 4 squares 3″ × 3″, cut a strip of fabric 3″ × 13″. If the cutting instructions call for 2 rectangles 3″ × 6″, cut a strip of fabric 3″ × 13″. Always cut the strip a little longer than necessary; this will allow you to square up the short end of the strip.

 Stay Organized

I find it very helpful to label each stack of cut pieces and keep them on an extra cutting mat. Then when I carry the mat to my sewing table, I am not confused when stitching the pieces together.

sewing

I've used several quick and easy methods to make the blocks and quilts in this book. They're accurate and a great time-saver. Once you try them, I'm sure you'll find that your quilts go together easier and faster than ever before.

When working with squares and rectangles, you often need to draw a thin pencil line diagonally through the piece in order to sew it to the next piece. DO NOT sew precisely on the drawn pencil line. You should sew one or two thread widths to the right of it to obtain a scant ¼″ seam allowance. This ensures that the piece will be the correct size after pressing. If you sew exactly on the pencil line, the piece will likely be too small after pressing.

Stitch just to right of pencil line.

SEWING ON THE DIAGONAL USING A SQUARE AND A RECTANGLE

Step One

On the wrong side of the fabric, draw a diagonal line across the square. With right sides together, place the square on the rectangle. Stitch one or two thread widths to the right of the pencil line.

Draw pencil line.

Align and stitch.

Step Two

Press the square according to the pressing arrows in the block instructions. Carefully lay the pieces on a cutting mat. Using a ruler and rotary cutter, trim ¼″ away from the stitching line. You will have 2 triangle-shaped pieces of fabric left over. Discard these or save them for another project.

Trim ¼″ from stitching line.

Drawing and Cutting Long Lines

If you don't have a 4″ × 36″ OmniEdge ruler, butt or tape two rulers together to get the length needed to draw the diagonal line on Unit 2 of the big Star blocks. Use the two rulers again after sewing Unit 2 to Unit 1 to trim ¼″ from the stitching line.

SEWING ON THE DIAGONAL USING TWO RECTANGLES

Step One

In order to draw a pencil line on a rectangle, position the top rectangle a little away from the edge of the rectangle that is beneath it, right sides together.

Align the top edge of the upper rectangle with the top edge of the lower rectangle. This allows you to see where to draw the diagonal pencil line.

Draw a pencil line from the upper corner diagonally to where the rectangles meet (45°).

Align and draw pencil line.

Step Two

Move the top rectangle so the edges of the 2 rectangles are even. Sew, press, and trim ¼″ from the stitching line.

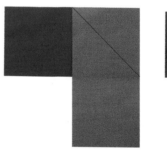

Align edges.

Stitch and trim.

After you sew the 2 rectangles together, the strip should be straight, not jagged looking. If the strips aren't straight, you'll have trouble later on when sewing 2 strips together.

Incorrect

Correct

NO-FAIL SEWING

Sewing Star quilt blocks has never been easier! Straight sewing is all that's required. In this section I will share some of my special hints and tips for making these quick and easy big Stars.

Seam Allowance

I find it's best to use a scant $\frac{1}{4}$″ seam allowance (unless otherwise noted) when piecing quilts. Using a scant seam allowance ensures that the units/blocks are true to size, because you regain the small amount of fabric that is lost due to the thickness of the sewing thread and the resulting "hump" that is created by pressing the seam allowances to one side.

Sewing Units Together

If your seam allowance is not a scant $\frac{1}{4}$″, you will have problems when creating Units 1 and 2. The A and B pieces will not fit the pieced units correctly. Take time to make certain your seam allowance is accurate. Your Units 1 and 2 should match to create accurate quarter Star blocks. Refer to the chart for the correct unfinished sizes of Units 1 and 2.

Unfinished Sizes of Unit 1 and Unit 2	
Wallhanging	$15\frac{7}{8}$″ × $15\frac{7}{8}$″
Lap	$26\frac{3}{4}$″ × $26\frac{3}{4}$″
Queen	$31\frac{1}{4}$″ × $31\frac{1}{4}$″
King	$37\frac{5}{8}$″ × $37\frac{5}{8}$″

 No-Fail Sewing Tips

Follow these hints when sewing diagonal seams and piecing. You will get perfect results every time.

■ Use a mechanical pencil with a lead no more than 0.5mm in diameter for drawing diagonal lines on light fabric, and use an ultra-fine-point black Sharpie for dark fabrics. Do not use a regular pencil. It will become dull very quickly, and the pencil line will be wider and bolder than desired.

■ Keep sharp needles in your sewing machine. A dull needle will distort the first few stitches.

■ A single-hole or straight-stitch throat plate is also helpful. It keeps the needle from pushing the corner of the square into the hole of a zigzag throat plate, which has a larger opening.

■ When sewing diagonally through a square or rectangle, start sewing on a scrap piece of fabric first, then continue sewing into the adjacent square or rectangle. This will help prevent distortion of the first one or two stitches.

■ Try piecing with an open-toe walking foot. The open toe will allow you to see where to sew *next to* the pencil line. The walking foot ensures that the two layers of fabric will feed through evenly. I do all my machine piecing on a Bernina with an open-toe walking foot.

■ The needle-stop down feature on the sewing machine is very helpful when piecing. It keeps the fabric in place when you stop sewing momentarily. Use this feature if your machine has it.

■ Press the diagonally sewn seam flat to "set" the stitches. This prevents distortion of the seam and pieces. Next press the seam allowance to one side. Then trim off the excess fabric.

■ If you're unsure whether the diamonds in your big Star block will align properly when you sew two units together, do a basting stitch between the diamonds first. Open up the units to see if the diamonds meet. Once you're satisfied, sew the entire seam using a normal stitch length.

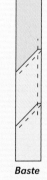

Baste between diamonds.

■ When adding borders to your block or sewing it into the quilt top, make sure the center seam (the one you sewed last) runs horizontal in the quilt. It will make for a more pleasing look.

Horizontal center seam

perfect piecing for star blocks

There are two secrets to getting perfectly pieced Star blocks with perfectly aligned seams: pressing and pinning.

PRESSING AND PINNING FOR PERFECTION

Sewing Unit 1 to Unit 2 creates one quarter of the Star block. It's very important to pin along the diagonal line where the seams butt together and along the outside edges. This is especially helpful when working with the big queen- and king-size blocks. This will keep the pieces from shifting while you are sewing Unit 1 to Unit 2. The following diagrams show you how the seam allowances should look on the wrong side of the block.

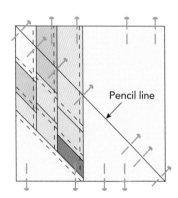

Pencil line

Wrong side of Unit 2 on top of Unit 1

Pin Unit 1 to Unit 2.

my favorite things

I use a Schmetz Jeans/Denim 70/10 needle for sewing. Don't be fooled by the words Jeans/Denim. The point of this needle is very sharp and it will give you a perfect top and bobbin stitch.

When sewn, pressed, and trimmed, your quarter Star block will look like the diagram below on the wrong side. In the block pattern instructions, the pressing is always the same when sewing Unit 1 to Unit 2 and when joining quarter blocks together to make a half Star block.

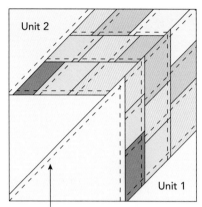

Unit 2

Unit 1

Unit 1 and 2 seam forms quarter of a star.

One-quarter Star

When you sew two quarter blocks together, you'll form half a Star block. When you place the quarter blocks right sides together, you'll notice that the seam allowances on the two quarters are pressed in opposite directions. This allows you to easily butt the seams together. After sewing the seam, turn the half block over. Look at the four diamonds that form half the star on the right side of the block, and you'll see that every other diamond point is slightly recessed, and the opposite diamonds are slightly raised. This is correct and will allow you to butt the seams together when sewing the two halves of the block. This will also give you a perfect center seam.

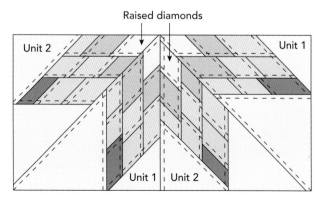

Raised diamonds

Unit 2 · · · · · · · · · · · · · · · · · · · Unit 1

Unit 1 · Unit 2

One-half Star

To complete the block, first pin the two halves together at each end. This will keep the edges of the block even. Next, butt the center seams so the raised diamonds fall into the recessed diamonds. Place a pin about $^1/_{16}''$ *ahead* of the butted seams. Do not pin directly in the seam intersection. If you do, you'll separate the butted seams, and the center of the star won't match precisely. Finally, before sewing place additional pins along the center seam where the rest of the diamonds meet.

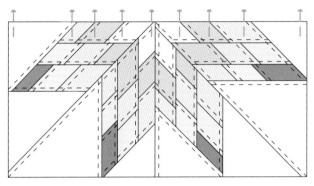

Pin two halves together.

Fine silk pins will allow you to pin your pieces together without creating a hump. Try using Collins Silk Pins (C104) by Prym-Dritz Corp.

 No-Fail Pressing Tips

I've been talking about and demonstrating good pressing habits since 1987. I truly believe that careful pressing is one of the reasons I've been able to make award-winning quilts. I feel so strongly about this part of quiltmaking that I always include pressing arrows with my pattern diagrams. If you follow these pressing arrows, you should be able to butt most of your pieces together to accurately align and stitch them. This will help keep your blocks square.

Here are a few other pressing tips:

■ Be sure to press each seam allowance before continuing to sew more pieces to the unit.

■ If you use steam, be extra careful when pressing. I normally don't use steam when piecing. I find it tends to distort many of the smaller pieces.

■ Use the cotton setting on your iron. If this doesn't seem hot enough, set it one notch higher. After a piece has been pressed, it should lie fairly flat on the ironing board.

■ To get stubborn seam allowances to lie flat, place a tiny piece of $^1/_4''$-wide Steam-A-Seam 2 under the seam allowance and press. This will fuse the seam allowance in place.

how to use the charts

YARDAGE AND CUTTING CHARTS FOR THE STAR BLOCKS

Yardage and cutting charts are provided with each Star block. The cutting charts for the blocks list the cut size of each piece, in inches. Single measurements indicate the size of a cut square (5 = 5″ × 5′). All yardages given are based on fabric that has 40″ of usable width.

I've overestimated the yardage needed by a small factor to allow for preshrinking the fabric and squaring up. All pieces, unless otherwise noted on the pattern, are cut *crosswise grain. This is very important because all yardages were calculated for cutting crosswise.*

CUTTING

Piece	Color	Number To Cut	Finished Size Stars			
			Wallhanging 30¾″ Square	Lap 52½″ Square	Queen 61½″ Square	King 74¼″ Square
A		8	9½ × 15⅞	15⅞ × 26¾	18½ × 31¼	22¼ × 37⅝
B		8	6⅞	11⅜	13¼	15⅞
C		8	2⅝ × 15⅞	4⅛ × 26¾	4¾ × 31¼	5⅝ × 37⅝
D		8	4¾ × 9⅞	7¾ × 16½	9 × 19¼	10¾ × 23⅛
E		16	2⅝ × 5⅝	4⅛ × 9¼	4¾ × 10¾	5⅝ × 12⅞
F		16	2⅝ × 7¾	4⅛ × 12⅞	4¾ × 15	5⅝ × 18

IMPORTANT NOTE: Cut all pieces crosswise grain except A for the wallhanging, lap, and queen size. To cut these pieces, see page 13.

YARDAGE NEEDED

		Wallhanging	Lap	Queen	King
A, B		1½	4¼	5	7⅜
C, D		¾	2⅛	2½	4⅛
E		⅜	¾	1	1¼
F		½	1	1⅜	1½

See How to Cut Background Piece A on page 13 for the most efficient use of your fabric when cutting the A pieces.

Use the smaller dimension to determine the width of the strip you need to cut. For example, if the cutting instructions call for 2 rectangles 2⅝″ × 15⅞″, cut a 2⅝″ × 40″ strip and then recut into 2 rectangles 15⅞″.

YARDAGE AND CUTTING CHARTS FOR THE QUILT MAPS

I've also overestimated the yardage needed for each Quilt Map to ensure that you will have enough fabric. I've given the exact length needed for each border, but make sure you measure your Star block and the center of your quilt before cutting the borders. Your sewing or seam allowance may be slightly different from mine, and you'll need to cut the borders to match the size of your quilt top.

WALLHANGING QUILT YARDAGE

Item	Color	Quantity Needed
* Inner Border (A)		⅜ yard
* Outer Border (B)		⅝ yard
Cornerstones (C)		¼ yard
Binding		½ yard
* Backing (D, E)		1⅜ yards

CUTTING

Item	Color	# To Cut	Size
A		4	2½″ × 31¼″
B		4	4¼″ × 31¼″
C		4	6¼″ × 6¼″
D	Backing	1	19″ × 46½″
E	Backing	1	19″ × 28″

Based on cutting crosswise grain of the fabric. Backing yardage is based on using part of the bonus cut-offs.

HOW TO CUT BACKGROUND PIECE A

The following illustrations show the best way to maximize the background fabric when cutting the A pieces for the Star blocks.

Wallhanging

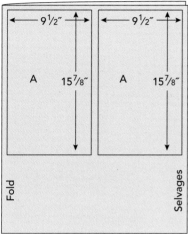

9½″ 9½″
A 15⅞″ A 15⅞″
Fold Selvages

Two layers of fabric.
Repeat 2 times.

Lap

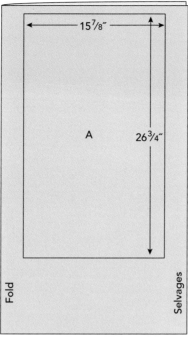

15⅞″
A 26¾″
Fold Selvages

Two layers of fabric.
Repeat 4 times.

Queen

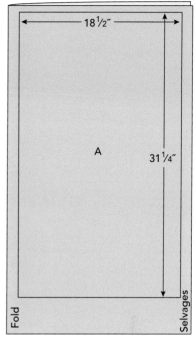

18½″
A 31¼″
Fold Selvages

Two layers of fabric.
Repeat 4 times.

King

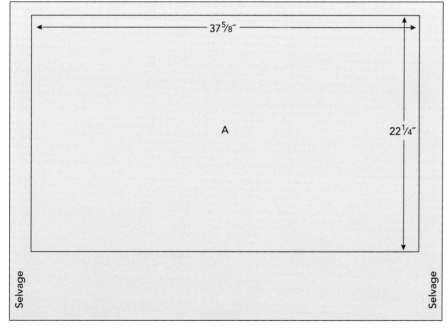

37⅝″
A 22¼″
Selvage Selvage

One layer of fabric.
Repeat 8 times.

✹ Cutting Backing and Binding

A piecing diagram for the backing using the large bonus cut-offs is included with each Quilt Map. The backing is 4″ larger than the size of the quilt for the wallhanging, 6″ larger for the lap and queen, and 8″ larger for the king-size quilt. For longarm quilting machines, the backing should be 10″ larger than the size of the quilt; you will need to add extra fabric.

In all the yardage charts, I allowed 3″ strips for binding to allow for individual preferences. I usually cut 2⅛″ strips for double-fold binding.

blocks 1-14

CUTTING

Piece	Color	Number To Cut	Finished Size Stars			
			Wallhanging 30¾" Square	Lap 52½" Square	Queen 61½" Square	King 74¼" Square
A	☐	8	9½ × 15⅞	15⅞ × 26¾	18½ × 31¼	22¼ × 37⅝
B	☐	8	6⅞	11⅜	13¼	15⅞
C	▦	4	2⅝ × 15⅞	4⅛ × 26¾	4¾ × 31¼	5⅝ × 37⅝
D	▦	4	6⅞ × 9⅞	11⅜ × 16½	13¼ × 19¼	15⅞ × 23⅛
E	☐	4	2⅝ × 15⅞	4⅛ × 26¾	4¾ × 31¼	5⅝ × 37⅝
F	☐	4	6⅞ × 9⅞	11⅜ × 16½	13¼ × 19¼	15⅞ × 23⅛
G	■	4	2⅝ × 15⅞	4⅛ × 26¾	4¾ × 31¼	5⅝ × 37⅝
H	■	4	6⅞ × 9⅞	11⅜ × 16½	13¼ × 19¼	15⅞ × 23⅛

IMPORTANT NOTE: Cut all pieces crosswise grain except A for the wallhanging, lap, and queen size. To cut these pieces, see page 13.

YARDAGE NEEDED

		Wallhanging	Lap	Queen	King
A, B	☐	1½	4¼	5	7⅜
C, D	▦	⅝	1½	1¾	3
E, F	☐	⅝	1½	1¾	3
G, H	■	⅝	1½	1¾	3

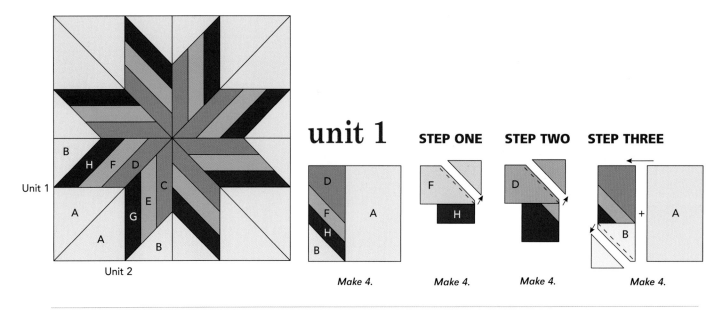

Unit 1

Unit 2

unit 1

STEP ONE **STEP TWO** **STEP THREE**

Make 4. *Make 4.* *Make 4.* *Make 4.*

unit 2

STEP ONE **STEP TWO**

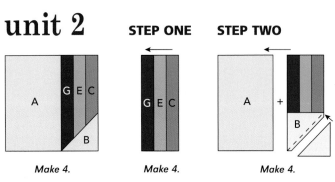

Make 4. *Make 4.* *Make 4.*

block assembly

STEP ONE

Draw a diagonal line on the WRONG SIDE of all Unit 2s,
as shown. Place Unit 2, WRONG SIDE up, on top of Unit 1.
Align, sew, press, and trim.

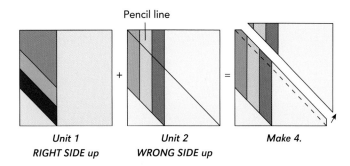

Pencil line

Unit 1
RIGHT SIDE up
+
Unit 2
WRONG SIDE up
=
Make 4.

STEP TWO

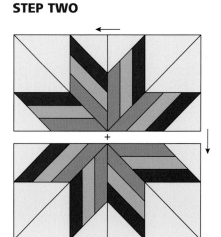

+

quilting designs for block 1

Wallhanging

Queen

block 2

CUTTING

Piece	Color	Number To Cut	Wallhanging 30¾″ Square	Lap 52½″ Square	Queen 61½″ Square	King 74¼″ Square
				Finished Size Stars		
A	☐	8	9½ × 15⅞	15⅞ × 26¾	18½ × 31¼	22¼ × 37⅝
B	☐	8	6⅞	11⅜	13¼	15⅞
C	■	4	2⅝ × 15⅞	4⅛ × 26¾	4¾ × 31¼	5⅝ × 37⅝
D	■	4	6⅞ × 9⅞	11⅜ × 16½	13¼ × 19¼	15⅞ × 23⅛
E	■	4	4¾ × 7¾	7¾ × 12⅞	9 × 15	10¾ × 18
F	■	4	2⅝ × 12⅞	4⅛ × 21⅝	4¾ × 25¼	5⅝ × 30⅜
G	■	8	4¾ × 12⅞	7¾ × 21⅝	9 × 25¼	10¾ × 30⅜

IMPORTANT NOTE: Cut all pieces crosswise grain except A for the wallhanging, lap, and queen size. To cut these pieces, see page 13.

YARDAGE NEEDED

		Wallhanging	Lap	Queen	King
A, B	☐	1½	4¼	5	7⅜
C, D, E, F	■	⅞	2⅜	2¾	4⅛
G	■	⅝	2	2⅜	2¾

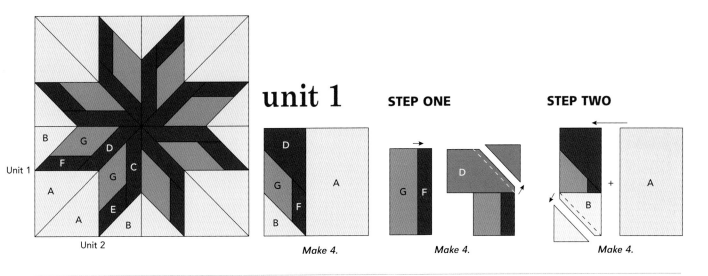

unit 1

STEP ONE

Make 4.

Make 4.

STEP TWO

Make 4.

unit 2

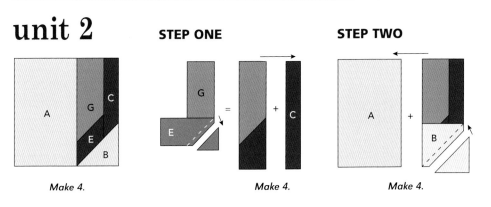

Make 4.

STEP ONE

Make 4.

STEP TWO

Make 4.

block assembly

STEP ONE

Draw a diagonal line on the WRONG SIDE of all Unit 2s, as shown. Place Unit 2, WRONG SIDE up, on top of Unit 1. Align, sew, press, and trim.

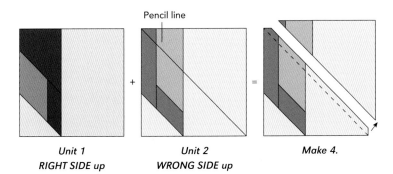

Pencil line

Unit 1
RIGHT SIDE up

Unit 2
WRONG SIDE up

Make 4.

STEP TWO

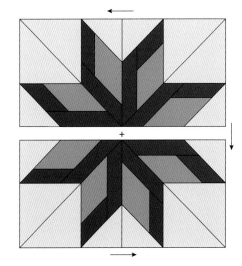

quilting designs for block 2

© Veronica Nurmi

Wallhanging

© Veronica Nurmi

Queen

block 3

CUTTING

Piece	Color	Number To Cut	Wallhanging 30³⁄₄″ Square	Lap 52¹⁄₂″ Square	Queen 61¹⁄₂″ Square	King 74¹⁄₄″ Square
				Finished Size Stars		
A	☐	8	9¹⁄₂ × 15⁷⁄₈	15⁷⁄₈ × 26³⁄₄	18¹⁄₂ × 31¹⁄₄	22¹⁄₄ × 37⁵⁄₈
B	☐	8	6⁷⁄₈	11³⁄₈	13¹⁄₄	15⁷⁄₈
C	■	12	2⁵⁄₈ × 5⁵⁄₈	4¹⁄₈ × 9¹⁄₄	4³⁄₄ × 10³⁄₄	5⁵⁄₈ × 12⁷⁄₈
D	■	8	2⁵⁄₈ × 9⁷⁄₈	4¹⁄₈ × 16¹⁄₂	4³⁄₄ × 19¹⁄₄	5⁵⁄₈ × 23¹⁄₈
E	■	8	2⁵⁄₈ × 7³⁄₄	4¹⁄₈ × 12⁷⁄₈	4³⁄₄ × 15	5⁵⁄₈ × 18
F	■	8	2⁵⁄₈ × 5⁵⁄₈	4¹⁄₈ × 9¹⁄₄	4³⁄₄ × 10³⁄₄	5⁵⁄₈ × 12⁷⁄₈
G	■	4	6⁷⁄₈ × 15⁷⁄₈	11³⁄₈ × 26³⁄₄	13¹⁄₄ × 31¹⁄₄	15⁷⁄₈ × 37⁵⁄₈

IMPORTANT NOTE: Cut all pieces crosswise grain except A for the wallhanging, lap, and queen size. To cut these pieces, see page 13.

YARDAGE NEEDED

		Wallhanging	Lap	Queen	King
A, B	☐	1¹⁄₂	4¹⁄₄	5	7³⁄₈
C, D	■	¹⁄₂	1	1¹⁄₄	2¹⁄₈
E, F	■	¹⁄₂	³⁄₄	1¹⁄₈	1³⁄₈
G	■	⁵⁄₈	1⁵⁄₈	2	2³⁄₈

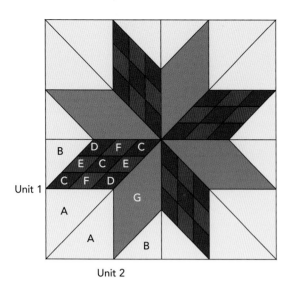

Unit 1
Unit 2

unit 1

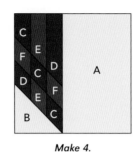

Make 4.

STEP ONE

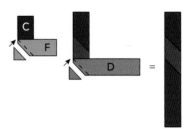

Make 4.

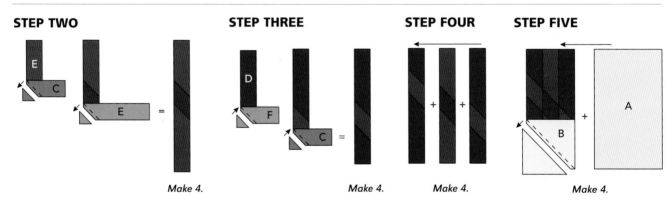

STEP TWO
Make 4.

STEP THREE
Make 4.

STEP FOUR
Make 4.

STEP FIVE
Make 4.

unit 2

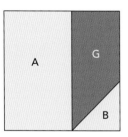

Make 4.

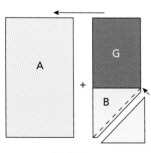

Make 4.

block assembly

STEP ONE

Draw a diagonal line on the WRONG SIDE of all Unit 2s as shown. Place Unit 2, WRONG SIDE up, on top of Unit 1. Align, sew, press, and trim.

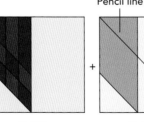

Pencil line

Unit 1
RIGHT SIDE up

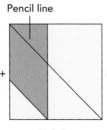

Unit 2
WRONG SIDE up

Make 4.

STEP TWO

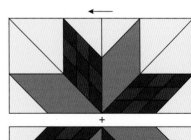

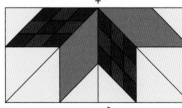

quilting designs for block 3

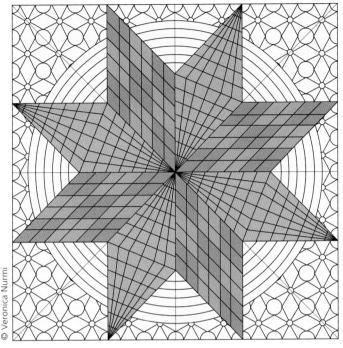

Wallhanging

Queen

block 4

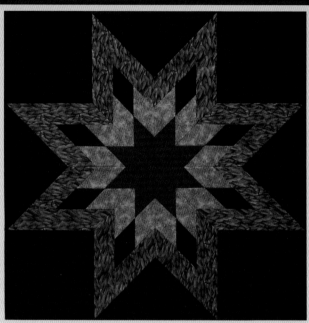

CUTTING

Piece	Color	Number To Cut	Finished Size Stars			
			Wallhanging 30¾″ Square	Lap 52½″ Square	Queen 61½″ Square	King 74¼″ Square
A	☐	8	9½ × 15⅞	15⅞ × 26¾	18½ × 31¼	22¼ × 37⅝
B	☐	8	6⅞	11⅜	13¼	15⅞
C	■	8	2⅝ × 5⅝	4⅛ × 9¼	4¾ × 10¾	5⅝ × 12⅞
D	■	16	2⅝ × 7¾	4⅛ × 12⅞	4¾ × 15	5⅝ × 18
E	■	8	2⅝ × 5⅝	4⅛ × 9¼	4¾ × 10¾	5⅝ × 12⅞
F	■	8	4¾ × 9⅞	7¾ × 16½	9 × 19¼	10¾ × 23⅛
G	■	8	2⅝ × 15⅞	4⅛ × 26¾	4¾ × 31¼	5⅝ × 37⅝

IMPORTANT NOTE: Cut all pieces crosswise grain except A for the wallhanging, lap, and queen size. To cut these pieces, see page 13.

YARDAGE NEEDED

		Wallhanging	Lap	Queen	King
A, B	☐	1½	4¼	5	7⅜
C	■	¼	½	⅝	¾
D	■	½	⅞	1⅜	1½
E	■	¼	½	⅝	¾
F, G	■	¾	2⅛	2⅜	4⅛

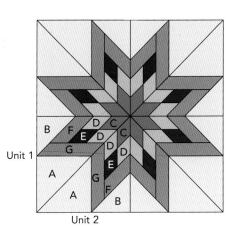

Unit 1
Unit 2

unit 1

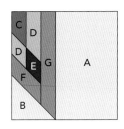

Make 4.

STEP ONE

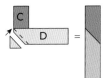 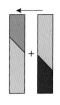

Make 4.

STEP TWO

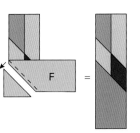

Make 4.

STEP THREE

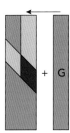

Make 4.

STEP FOUR

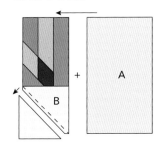

Make 4.

unit 2

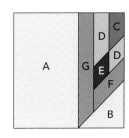

Make 4.

STEP ONE

Make 4.

STEP TWO

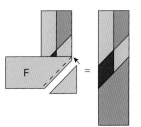

Make 4.

STEP THREE

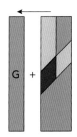

Make 4.

---

block assembly

STEP FOUR

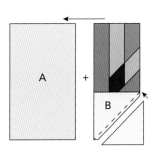

Make 4.

STEP ONE

Draw a diagonal line on the WRONG SIDE of all Unit 2s, as shown. Place Unit 2, WRONG SIDE up, on top of Unit 1. Align, sew, press, and trim.

Pencil line

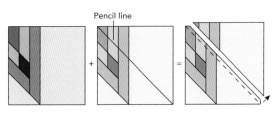

Unit 1
RIGHT SIDE up

Unit 2
WRONG SIDE up

Make 4.

STEP TWO

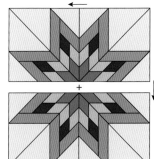
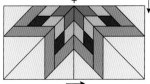

quilting designs for block 4

© Veronica Nurmi

Wallhanging

© Veronica Nurmi

Queen

block **5**

CUTTING

Piece	Color	Number To Cut	Wallhanging 30¾″ Square	Lap 52½″ Square	Queen 61½″ Square	King 74¼″ Square
				Finished Size Stars		
A	☐	8	9½ × 15⅞	15⅞ × 26¾	18½ × 31¼	22¼ × 37⅝
B	☐	8	6⅞	11⅜	13¼	15⅞
C	■	8	4¾ × 10¾	7¾ × 18	9 × 21	10¾ × 25¼
D	■	8	4¾	7¾	9	10¾
E	■	8	2⅝ × 10¾	4⅛ × 18	4¾ × 21	5⅝ × 25¼
F	■	8	2⅝ × 5⅝	4⅛ × 9¼	4¾ × 10¾	5⅝ × 12⅞
G	■	8	2⅝ × 4¾	4⅛ × 7¾	4¾ × 9	5⅝ × 10¾
H	■	8	4¾ × 5⅝	7¾ × 9¼	9 × 10¾	10¾ × 12⅞

IMPORTANT NOTE: Cut all pieces crosswise grain except A for the wallhanging, lap, and queen size. To cut these pieces, see page 13.

YARDAGE NEEDED

		Wallhanging	Lap	Queen	King
A, B	☐	1½	4¼	5	7⅜
C	■	⅝	1⅛	2½	2¾
D, E, F	■	¾	1½	2⅜	3
G, H	■	½	1	1⅜	1¾

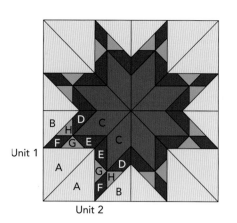

unit 1

STEP ONE

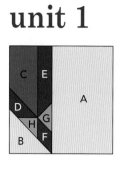

Make 4.

STEP TWO

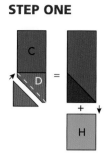

Make 4.

Make 4.

Unit 1

Unit 2

STEP THREE

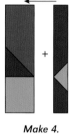

Make 4.

STEP FOUR

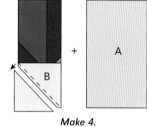

Make 4.

unit 2

STEP ONE

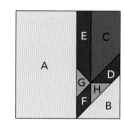

Make 4.

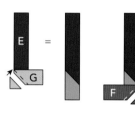

Make 4.

STEP TWO

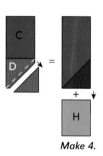

Make 4.

STEP THREE

Make 4.

STEP FOUR

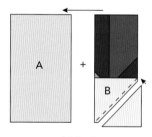

Make 4.

block assembly

STEP ONE

Draw a diagonal line on the WRONG SIDE of all
Unit 2s, as shown. Place Unit 2, WRONG SIDE up,
on top of Unit 1. Align, sew, press, and trim.

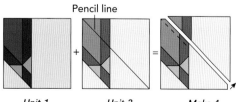

Pencil line

Unit 1
RIGHT SIDE up

Unit 2
WRONG SIDE up

Make 4.

STEP TWO

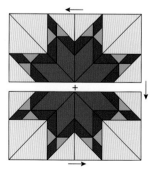

quilting designs for block 5

Wallhanging

Queen

block 6

CUTTING

Piece	Color	Number To Cut	Finished Size Stars			
			Wallhanging 30¾″ Square	Lap 52½″ Square	Queen 61½″ Square	King 74¼″ Square
A	▢	8	9½ × 15⅞	15⅞ × 26¾	18½ × 31¼	22¼ × 37⅝
B	▢	8	6⅞	11⅜	13¼	15⅞
C	▨	8	2⅝ × 5⅝	4⅛ × 9¼	4¾ × 10¾	5⅝ × 12⅞
D	▢	8	2⅝ × 5⅝	4⅛ × 9¼	4¾ × 10¾	5⅝ × 12⅞
E	▢	8	2⅝ × 7¾	4⅛ × 12⅞	4¾ × 15	5⅝ × 18
F	■	16	2⅝ × 9⅞	4⅛ × 16½	4¾ × 19¼	5⅝ × 23⅛
G	■	8	2⅝ × 5⅝	4⅛ × 9¼	4¾ × 10¾	5⅝ × 12⅞
H	▢	8	2⅝ × 5⅝	4⅛ × 9¼	4¾ × 10¾	5⅝ × 12⅞
I	▢	8	2⅝ × 7¾	4⅛ × 12⅞	4¾ × 15	5⅝ × 18
J	■	8	2⅝ × 5⅝	4⅛ × 9¼	4¾ × 10¾	5⅝ × 12⅞

IMPORTANT NOTE: Cut all pieces crosswise grain except A for the wallhanging, lap, and queen size. To cut these pieces, see page 13.

YARDAGE NEEDED

		Wallhanging	Lap	Queen	King
A, B	▢	1½	4¼	5	7⅜
C	▨	⅜	½	⅝	¾
D, E	▢	½	⅞	1¼	1⅜
F, G	■	⅝	1⅜	1⅝	3¼
H, I	▢	½	⅞	1¼	1⅜
J	■	⅜	½	⅝	¾

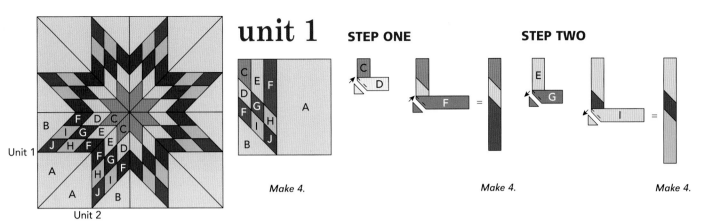

unit 1

STEP ONE

Make 4.

STEP TWO

Make 4.

Make 4.

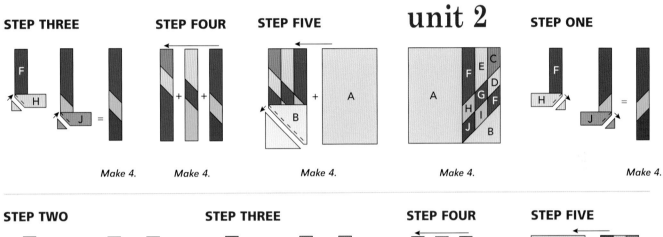

STEP THREE

Make 4.

STEP FOUR

Make 4.

STEP FIVE

Make 4.

unit 2

Make 4.

STEP ONE

Make 4.

STEP TWO

Make 4.

STEP THREE

Make 4.

STEP FOUR

Make 4.

STEP FIVE

Make 4.

block assembly

STEP ONE

Draw a diagonal line on the WRONG SIDE of all Unit 2s, as shown. Place Unit 2, WRONG SIDE up, on top of Unit 1. Align, sew, press, and trim.

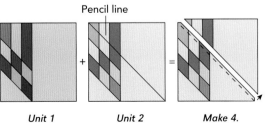

Pencil line

Unit 1
RIGHT SIDE up

Unit 2
WRONG SIDE up

Make 4.

STEP TWO

quilting designs for block 6

Wallhanging

Queen

block 7

CUTTING

Piece	Color	Number To Cut	Wallhanging 30¾″ Square	Lap 52½″ Square	Queen 61½″ Square	King 74¼″ Square
				Finished Size Stars		
A	☐	8	9½ × 15⅞	15⅞ × 26¾	18½ × 31¼	22¼ × 37⅝
B	☐	8	6⅞	11⅜	13¼	15⅞
C	☐	16	2⅝ × 9⅞	4⅛ × 16½	4¾ × 19¼	5⅝ × 23⅛
D	☐	8	2⅝ × 5⅝	4⅛ × 9¼	4¾ × 10¾	5⅝ × 12⅞
E	▩	8	2⅝ × 8⅝	4⅛ × 14⅜	4¾ × 16¾	5⅝ × 20⅛
F	▩	8	2⅝ × 7¾	4⅛ × 12⅞	4¾ × 15	5⅝ × 18
G	■	8	2⅝ × 7¾	4⅛ × 12⅞	4¾ × 15	5⅝ × 18
H	■	8	2⅝ × 8⅝	4⅛ × 14⅜	4¾ × 16¾	5⅝ × 20⅛

IMPORTANT NOTE: Cut all pieces crosswise grain except A for the wallhanging, lap, and queen size. To cut these pieces, see page 13.

YARDAGE NEEDED

		Wallhanging	Lap	Queen	King
A, B, C, D	☐	2¼	5½	6⅝	10⅛
E, F	▩	½	1	1⅜	2⅛
G, H	■	½	1	1⅜	2⅛

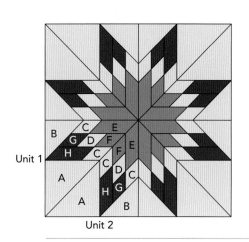

Unit 1

Unit 2

unit 1

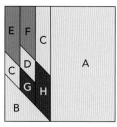

Make 4.

STEP ONE

Make 4.

STEP TWO

Make 4.

STEP THREE

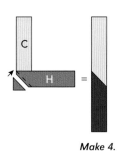

Make 4.

STEP FOUR

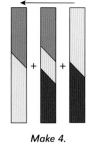

Make 4.

STEP FIVE

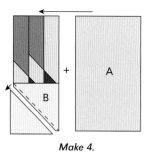

Make 4.

unit 2

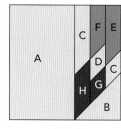

Make 4.

STEP ONE

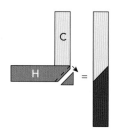

Make 4.

STEP TWO

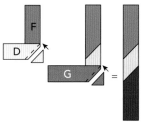

Make 4.

STEP THREE

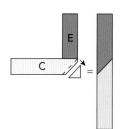

Make 4.

STEP FOUR

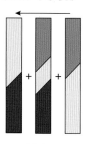

Make 4.

STEP FIVE

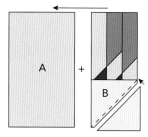

Make 4.

block assembly

STEP ONE

Draw a diagonal line on the WRONG SIDE of all Unit 2s, as shown. Place Unit 2, WRONG SIDE up, on top of Unit 1. Align, sew, press, and trim.

Unit 1
RIGHT SIDE up

Pencil line

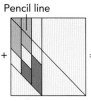

Unit 2
WRONG SIDE up

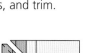

Make 4.

STEP TWO

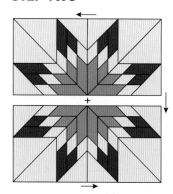

quilting designs for block 7

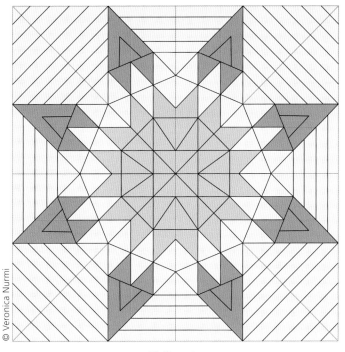

Wallhanging

Queen

block 8

CUTTING

Piece	Color	Number To Cut	Finished Size Stars			
			Wallhanging 30¾″ Square	Lap 52½″ Square	Queen 61½″ Square	King 74¼″ Square
A	▫	8	9½ × 15⅞	15⅞ × 26¾	18½ × 31¼	22¼ × 37⅝
B	▫	8	6⅞	11⅜	13¼	15⅞
C	■	4	2⅝ × 15⅞	4⅛ × 26¾	4¾ × 31¼	5⅝ × 37⅝
D	■	4	2⅝ × 10¾	4⅛ × 18	4¾ × 21	5⅝ × 25¼
E	■	8	2⅝ × 9⅞	4⅛ × 16½	4¾ × 19¼	5⅝ × 23⅛
F	■	4	2⅝ × 6½	4⅛ × 10¾	4¾ × 12½	5⅝ × 15
G	■	4	2⅝ × 11⅝	4⅛ × 19½	4¾ × 22¾	5⅝ × 27⅜
H	■	8	2⅝ × 5⅝	4⅛ × 9¼	4¾ × 10¾	5⅝ × 12⅞
I	■	8	2⅝ × 5⅝	4⅛ × 9¼	4¾ × 10¾	5⅝ × 12⅞
J	■	8	2⅝ × 7¾	4⅛ × 12⅞	4¾ × 15	5⅝ × 18
K	■	4	4¾	7¾	9	10¾
L	■	4	6⅞	11⅜	13¼	15⅞

IMPORTANT NOTE: Cut all pieces crosswise grain except A for the wallhanging, lap, and queen size. To cut these pieces, see page 13.

YARDAGE NEEDED

		Wallhanging	Lap	Queen	King
A, B	▫	1½	4¼	5	7⅜
C, D, E, F, G, H	■	1	2⅛	3	4¼
I, J, K	■	⅝	1⅛	1⅝	2⅛
L	■	½	¾	⅞	1⅜

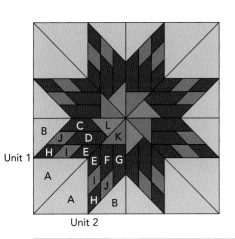

Unit 1

Unit 2

unit 1

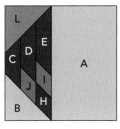

Make 4.

STEP ONE

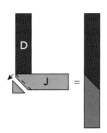

Make 4.

STEP TWO

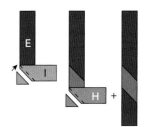

Make 4.

STEP THREE

Make 4.

STEP FOUR

Make 4.

STEP FIVE

Make 4.

unit 2

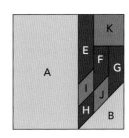

Make 4.

STEP ONE

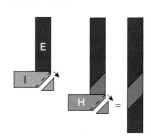

Make 4.

STEP TWO

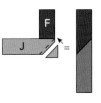

Make 4.

STEP THREE

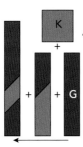

Make 4.

STEP FOUR

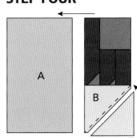

Make 4.

block assembly

STEP ONE

Draw a diagonal line on the WRONG SIDE of all Unit 2s, as shown. Place Unit 2, WRONG SIDE up, on top of Unit 1. Align, sew, press, and trim.

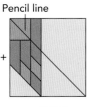

Pencil line

Unit 1
RIGHT SIDE up

Unit 2
WRONG SIDE up

Make 4.

STEP TWO

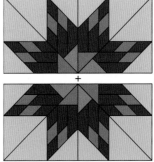

quilting designs for block 8

Wallhanging

Queen

block 9

CUTTING

Piece	Color	Number To Cut	Finished Size Stars Wallhanging 30³⁄₄″ Square	Lap 52¹⁄₂″ Square	Queen 61¹⁄₂″ Square	King 74¹⁄₄″ Square
A		8	9¹⁄₂ × 15⁷⁄₈	15⁷⁄₈ × 26³⁄₄	18¹⁄₂ × 31¹⁄₄	22¹⁄₄ × 37⁵⁄₈
B		8	6⁷⁄₈	11³⁄₈	13¹⁄₄	15⁷⁄₈
C		4	6⁷⁄₈ × 9⁷⁄₈	11³⁄₈ × 16¹⁄₂	13¹⁄₄ × 19¹⁄₄	15⁷⁄₈ × 23¹⁄₈
D		4	2⁵⁄₈ × 15⁷⁄₈	4¹⁄₈ × 26³⁄₄	4³⁄₄ × 31¹⁄₄	5⁵⁄₈ × 37⁵⁄₈
E		8	2⁵⁄₈ × 5⁵⁄₈	4¹⁄₈ × 9¹⁄₄	4³⁄₄ × 10³⁄₄	5⁵⁄₈ × 12⁷⁄₈
F		4	2⁵⁄₈ × 5⁵⁄₈	4¹⁄₈ × 9¹⁄₄	4³⁄₄ × 10³⁄₄	5⁵⁄₈ × 12⁷⁄₈
G		4	2⁵⁄₈ × 7³⁄₄	4¹⁄₈ × 12⁷⁄₈	4³⁄₄ × 15	5⁵⁄₈ × 18
H		8	2⁵⁄₈ × 9⁷⁄₈	4¹⁄₈ × 16¹⁄₂	4³⁄₄ × 19¹⁄₄	5⁵⁄₈ × 23¹⁄₈
I		4	2⁵⁄₈ × 7³⁄₄	4¹⁄₈ × 12⁷⁄₈	4³⁄₄ × 15	5⁵⁄₈ × 18
J		4	2⁵⁄₈ × 5⁵⁄₈	4¹⁄₈ × 9¹⁄₄	4³⁄₄ × 10³⁄₄	5⁵⁄₈ × 12⁷⁄₈
K		8	2⁵⁄₈ × 7³⁄₄	4¹⁄₈ × 12⁷⁄₈	4³⁄₄ × 15	5⁵⁄₈ × 18
L		4	2⁵⁄₈ × 9⁷⁄₈	4¹⁄₈ × 16¹⁄₂	4³⁄₄ × 19¹⁄₄	5⁵⁄₈ × 23¹⁄₈
M		4	2⁵⁄₈ × 5⁵⁄₈	4¹⁄₈ × 9¹⁄₄	4³⁄₄ × 10³⁄₄	5⁵⁄₈ × 12⁷⁄₈

IMPORTANT NOTE: Cut all pieces crosswise grain except A for the wallhanging, lap, and queen size. To cut these pieces, see page 13.

YARDAGE NEEDED

		Wallhanging	Lap	Queen	King
A, B		1¹⁄₂	4¹⁄₄	5	7³⁄₈
C, D, E		³⁄₄	1³⁄₄	2¹⁄₈	3¹⁄₂
F, G		³⁄₈	⁵⁄₈	⁷⁄₈	⁷⁄₈
H, I, J		¹⁄₂	1	1³⁄₈	2¹⁄₄
K, L, M		¹⁄₂	1	1³⁄₈	1⁷⁄₈

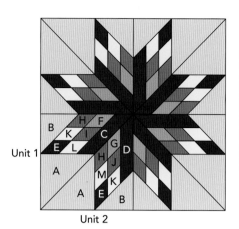

unit 1

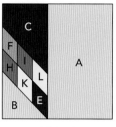

Make 4.

STEP ONE

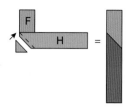

Make 4.

STEP TWO

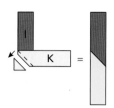

Make 4.

STEP THREE

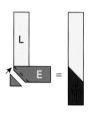

Make 4.

STEP FOUR

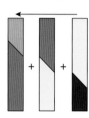

Make 4.

STEP FIVE

Make 4.

STEP SIX

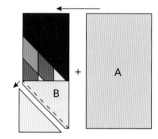

Make 4.

unit 2

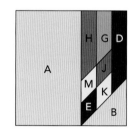

Make 4.

STEP ONE

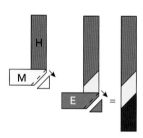

Make 4.

STEP TWO

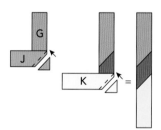

Make 4.

STEP THREE

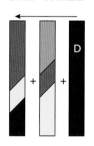

Make 4.

STEP FOUR

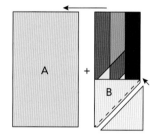

Make 4.

block assembly

STEP ONE

Draw a diagonal line on the WRONG SIDE of all Unit 2s, as shown. Place Unit 2, WRONG SIDE up, on top of Unit 1. Align, sew, press, and trim.

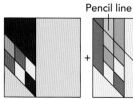

Unit 1
RIGHT SIDE up

Unit 2
WRONG SIDE up

Make 4.

STEP TWO

quilting designs for block 9

Wallhanging

Queen

block 10

CUTTING

Piece	Color	Number To Cut	Finished Size Stars			
			Wallhanging 30¾″ Square	**Lap** 52½″ Square	**Queen** 61½″ Square	**King** 74¼″ Square
A	☐	8	9½ × 15⅞	15⅞ × 26¾	18½ × 31¼	22¼ × 37⅝
B	☐	8	6⅞	11⅜	13¼	15⅞
C	☐	8	2⅝ × 5⅝	4⅛ × 9¼	4¾ × 10¾	5⅝ × 12⅞
D	■	8	2⅝ × 5⅝	4⅛ × 9¼	4¾ × 10¾	5⅝ × 12⅞
E	■	8	2⅝ × 9⅞	4⅛ × 16½	4¾ × 19¼	5⅝ × 23⅛
F	■	16	2⅝ × 9⅞	4⅛ × 16½	4¾ × 19¼	5⅝ × 23⅛
G	■	8	4¾ × 10¾	7¾ × 18	9 × 21	10¾ × 25¼

IMPORTANT NOTE: Cut all pieces crosswise grain except A for the wallhanging, lap, and queen size. To cut these pieces, see page 13.

YARDAGE NEEDED

		Wallhanging	Lap	Queen	King
A, B	☐	1½	4¼	5	7⅜
C	☐	⅜	½	⅝	¾
D, E	■	½	⅞	1¼	2
F	■	½	1⅛	1⅜	2¾
G	■	⅝	1¼	2⅜	2⅞

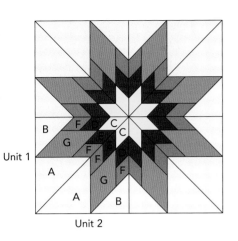

Unit 1

Unit 2

unit 1

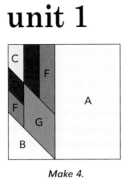

Make 4.

STEP ONE

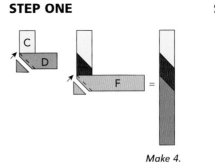

Make 4.

STEP TWO

E + F

Make 4.

STEP THREE

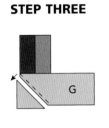

G

Make 4.

STEP FOUR

+

Make 4.

STEP FIVE

+ A

B

Make 4.

unit 2

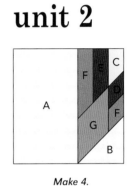

A

F E C
D
G F
B

Make 4.

STEP ONE

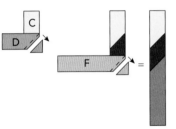

C
D
F =

Make 4.

STEP TWO

+ E

Make 4.

STEP THREE

G

Make 4.

STEP FOUR

+

Make 4.

STEP FIVE

A +

B

Make 4.

block assembly

STEP ONE

Draw a diagonal line on the WRONG SIDE of all Unit 2s, as shown. Place Unit 2, WRONG SIDE up, on top of Unit 1. Align, sew, press, and trim.

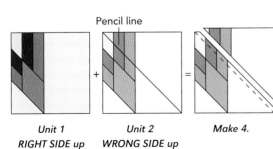

Pencil line

+ =

Unit 1
RIGHT SIDE up

Unit 2
WRONG SIDE up

Make 4.

STEP TWO

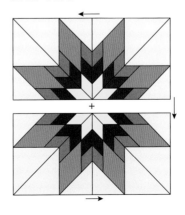

+

quilting designs for block 10

Wallhanging

Queen

block 11

CUTTING

Piece	Color	Number To Cut	Wallhanging 30³/₄″ Square	Finished Size Stars Lap 52¹/₂″ Square	Queen 61¹/₂″ Square	King 74¹/₄″ Square
A		8	9¹/₂ × 15⁷/₈	15⁷/₈ × 26³/₄	18¹/₂ × 31¹/₄	22¹/₄ × 37⁵/₈
B		8	6⁷/₈	11³/₈	13¹/₄	15⁷/₈
C		8	4³/₄ × 5⁵/₈	7³/₄ × 9¹/₄	9 × 10³/₄	10³/₄ × 12⁷/₈
D		8	2⁵/₈	4¹/₈	4³/₄	5⁵/₈
E		4	2⁵/₈ × 5⁵/₈	4¹/₈ × 9¹/₄	4³/₄ × 10³/₄	5⁵/₈ × 12⁷/₈
F		36	2⁵/₈ × 3¹/₂	4¹/₈ × 5⁵/₈	4³/₄ × 6¹/₂	5⁵/₈ × 7³/₄
G		4	1³/₄ × 6⁷/₈	2⁵/₈ × 11³/₈	3 × 13¹/₄	3¹/₂ × 15⁷/₈
H		36	2⁵/₈ × 3¹/₂	4¹/₈ × 5⁵/₈	4³/₄ × 6¹/₂	5⁵/₈ × 7³/₄
I		4	1³/₄ × 6⁷/₈	2⁵/₈ × 11³/₈	3 × 13¹/₄	3¹/₂ × 15⁷/₈
J		4	2⁵/₈ × 5⁵/₈	4¹/₈ × 9¹/₄	4³/₄ × 10³/₄	5⁵/₈ × 12⁷/₈

IMPORTANT NOTE: Cut all pieces crosswise grain except A for the wallhanging, lap, and queen size. To cut these pieces, see page 13.

YARDAGE NEEDED

		Wallhanging	Lap	Queen	King
A, B, C, D		1⁷/₈	4³/₄	5⁷/₈	8¹/₂
E, F, G		5/₈	1¹/₈	1³/₈	2¹/₈
H, I, J		5/₈	1¹/₈	1³/₈	2¹/₈

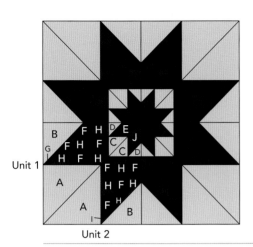

Unit 1

Unit 2

unit 1

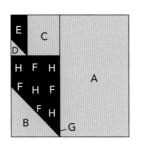

Make 4.

STEP ONE

Make 4.

STEP TWO

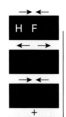

Make 4.

STEP THREE

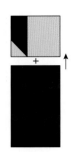

Make 4.

STEP FOUR

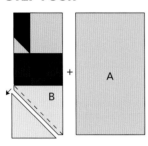

Make 4.

unit 2

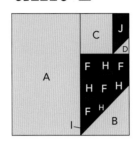

Make 4.

STEP ONE

Make 4.

STEP TWO

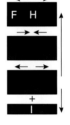

Make 4.

STEP THREE

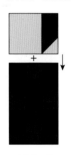

Make 4.

block assembly

STEP FOUR

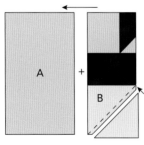

Make 4.

STEP ONE

Draw a diagonal line on the WRONG SIDE of all Unit 2s, as shown. Place Unit 2, WRONG SIDE up, on top of Unit 1. Align, sew, press, and trim.

Pencil line

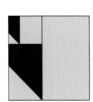 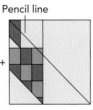

Unit 1
RIGHT SIDE up

Unit 2
WRONG SIDE up

Make 4.

STEP TWO

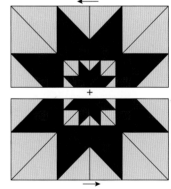

quilting designs for block 11

Wallhanging

Queen

block 12

CUTTING

Piece	Color	Number To Cut	Finished Size Stars			
			Wallhanging 30¾″ Square	Lap 52½″ Square	Queen 61½″ Square	King 74¼″ Square
A	☐	8	9½ × 15⅞	15⅞ × 26¾	18½ × 31¼	22¼ × 37⅝
B	☐	8	6⅞	11⅜	13¼	15⅞
C	◼	8	2⅝ × 15⅞	4⅛ × 26¾	4¾ × 31¼	5⅝ × 37⅝
D	◼	8	2⅝ × 5⅝	4⅛ × 9¼	4¾ × 10¾	5⅝ × 12⅞
E	◼	8	2⅝ × 7¾	4⅛ × 12⅞	4¾ × 15	5⅝ × 18
F	◼	8	2⅝ × 9⅞	4⅛ × 16½	4¾ × 19¼	5⅝ × 23⅛
G	◼	8	2⅝ × 5⅝	4⅛ × 9¼	4¾ × 10¾	5⅝ × 12⅞
H	◼	8	2⅝ × 5⅝	4⅛ × 9¼	4¾ × 10¾	5⅝ × 12⅞
I	◼	8	2⅝ × 7¾	4⅛ × 12⅞	4¾ × 15	5⅝ × 18

IMPORTANT NOTE: Cut all pieces crosswise grain except A for the wallhanging, lap, and queen size. To cut these pieces, see page 13.

YARDAGE NEEDED

		Wallhanging	Lap	Queen	King
A, B	☐	1½	4¼	5	7⅜
C, D	◼	⅝	1⅜	1¾	2
E	◼	⅜	⅝	¾	⅞
F, G	◼	½	1	1¼	2
H, I	◼	½	⅞	1⅛	1⅜

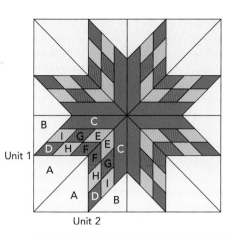

unit 1

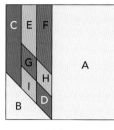

Make 4.

STEP ONE

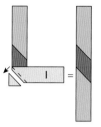

Make 4.

STEP TWO

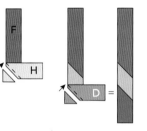

Make 4.   Make 4.

STEP THREE

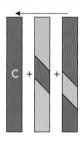

STEP FOUR

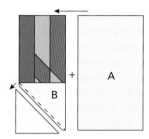

Make 4.

unit 2

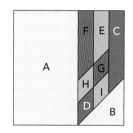

Make 4.

STEP ONE

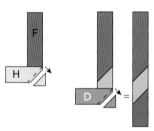

Make 4.

STEP TWO

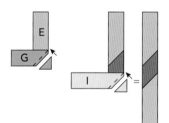

Make 4.

STEP THREE

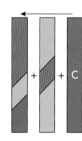

Make 4.

STEP FOUR

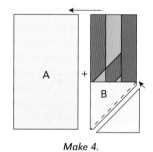

Make 4.

block assembly

STEP ONE

Draw a diagonal line on the WRONG SIDE of all Unit 2s, as shown. Place Unit 2, WRONG SIDE up, on top of Unit 1. Align, sew, press, and trim.

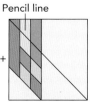

Pencil line

Unit 1
RIGHT SIDE up

Unit 2
WRONG SIDE up

Make 4.

STEP TWO

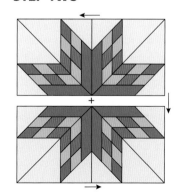

quilting designs for block 12

Wallhanging

Queen

block 13

CUTTING

Piece	Color	Number To Cut	Finished Size Stars			
			Wallhanging 30¾″ Square	Lap 52½″ Square	Queen 61½″ Square	King 74¼″ Square
A		8	9½ × 15⅞	15⅞ × 26¾	18½ × 31¼	22¼ × 37⅝
B		8	6⅞	11⅜	13¼	15⅞
C		8	2⅝ × 15⅞	4⅛ × 26¾	4¾ × 31¼	5⅝ × 37⅝
D		8	4¾ × 9⅞	7¾ × 16½	9 × 19¼	10¾ × 23⅛
E		16	2⅝ × 5⅝	4⅛ × 9¼	4¾ × 10¾	5⅝ × 12⅞
F		16	2⅝ × 7¾	4⅛ × 12⅞	4¾ × 15	5⅝ × 18

IMPORTANT NOTE: Cut all pieces crosswise grain except A for the wallhanging, lap, and queen size. To cut these pieces, see page 13.

YARDAGE NEEDED

		Wallhanging	Lap	Queen	King
A, B		1½	4¼	5	7⅜
C, D		¾	2⅛	2½	4⅛
E		⅜	¾	1	1¼
F		½	1	1⅜	1½

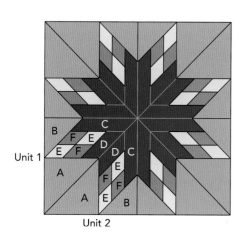

unit 1

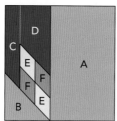

Make 4.

STEP ONE

Make 4.

STEP TWO

Make 4.

STEP THREE

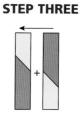

Make 4.

STEP FOUR

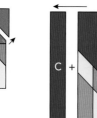

Make 4.

STEP FIVE

Make 4.

STEP SIX

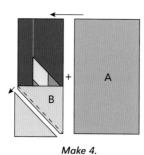

Make 4.

unit 2

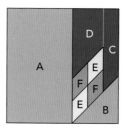

Make 4.

STEP ONE

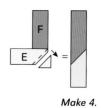

Make 4.

STEP TWO

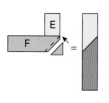

Make 4.

STEP THREE

Make 4.

STEP FOUR

Make 4.

STEP FIVE

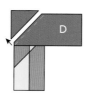

Make 4.

STEP SIX

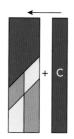

Make 4.

block assembly

STEP ONE

Draw a diagonal line on the WRONG SIDE of all
Unit 2s, as shown. Place Unit 2, WRONG SIDE up,
on top of Unit 1. Align, sew, press, and trim.

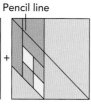

Pencil line

Unit 1
RIGHT SIDE up

Unit 2
WRONG SIDE up

Make 4.

STEP TWO

quilting designs for block 13

Wallhanging

Queen

block 14

CUTTING

Piece	Color	Number To Cut	Finished Size Stars			
			Wallhanging 30¾″ Square	Lap 52½″ Square	Queen 61½″ Square	King 74¼″ Square
A		8	9½ × 15⅞	15⅞ × 26¾	18½ × 31¼	22¼ × 37⅝
B		8	6⅞	11⅜	13¼	15⅞
C		24	2⅝ × 5⅝	4⅛ × 9¼	4¾ × 10¾	5⅝ × 12⅞
D		8	2⅝ × 12⅞	4⅛ × 21⅝	4¾ × 25¼	5⅝ × 30⅜
E		8	4¾ × 9⅞	7¾ × 16½	9 × 19¼	10¾ × 23⅛
F		16	2⅝ × 7¾	4⅛ × 12⅞	4¾ × 15	5⅝ × 18

IMPORTANT NOTE: Cut all pieces crosswise grain except A for the wallhanging, lap, and queen size. To cut these pieces, see page 13.

YARDAGE NEEDED

		Wallhanging	Lap	Queen	King
A, B		1½	4¼	5	7⅜
C		½	⅞	1⅜	1½
D, E		¾	2⅛	2⅜	4⅛
F		½	⅞	1⅜	1½

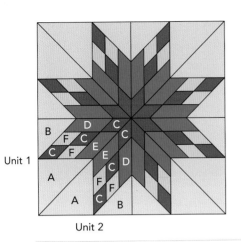

Unit 1

Unit 2

unit 1

STEP ONE

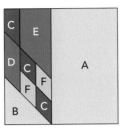

Make 4.

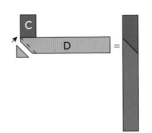

Make 4.

STEP TWO

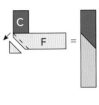

Make 4.

STEP THREE

Make 4.

STEP FOUR

Make 4.

STEP FIVE

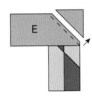

Make 4.

STEP SIX

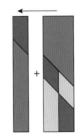

Make 4.

STEP SEVEN

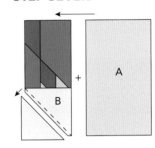

Make 4.

unit 2

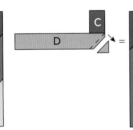

Make 4.

STEP ONE

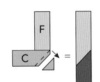

Make 4.

STEP TWO

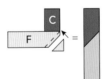

Make 4.

STEP THREE

Make 4.

STEP FOUR

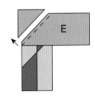

Make 4.

STEP FIVE

Make 4.

STEP SIX

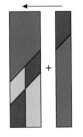

Make 4.

STEP SEVEN

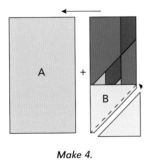

Make 4.

block assembly

STEP ONE

Draw a diagonal line on the WRONG SIDE of all Unit 2s, as shown. Place Unit 2, WRONG SIDE up, on top of Unit 1. Align, sew, press, and trim.

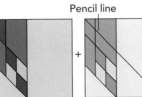

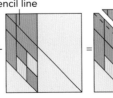

Pencil line

Unit 1
RIGHT SIDE up

Unit 2
WRONG SIDE up

Make 4.

STEP TWO

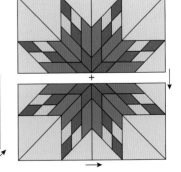

quilting designs for block 14

Wallhanging

© Veronica Nurmi

Queen

© Veronica Nurmi

quilts&projects

Yippee! It's time to work with the left-over bonus cut-offs. I knew from my previous book, *Stars by Magic*, that I'd have cut-offs, but nothing prepared me for the great wallhangings I'd be able to make. There were times I'd hurry and make the Star block simply because I wanted to see what I could do with the bonus cut-offs! Another exciting thing was realizing that I could make a wonderful pieced backing from the large triangles left over from sewing Unit 1 to Unit 2. When people see the backs of my quilts, they think I've spent hours designing and sewing the backing! Little do they know that I've spent only a few minutes sewing the cut-offs together and adding some border strips to make the piece large enough to use as the backing.

Buy Smart

Purchase extra fabric if you're going to make bonus wallhangings and backings. This will ensure that you have enough fabric for borders and so on.

no-fail tips and tricks for bonus cut-offs

SEWING BONUS CUT-OFFS

It's a lot easier to mark and sew the bonus cut-offs before trimming them from the Star block. I'll use parts of Block 4 to illustrate how to do this.

Step One

Draw a bonus pencil line ½" away from the original pencil line.

Step Two

Sew next to each of the pencil lines.

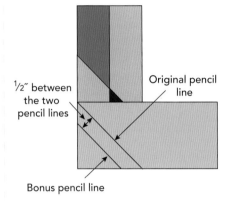

½" between the two pencil lines

Original pencil line

Bonus pencil line

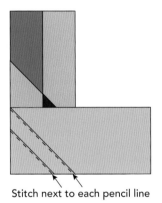

Stitch next to each pencil line

Step Three

Cut between the 2 stitching lines. The Star unit will have a ¼" seam allowance and the bonus cut-off will have a ¼" seam allowance.

This method works every time you want a bonus cut-off! Your biggest bonus cut-off will come from sewing Unit 1 to Unit 2. These cut-offs can be used for the bonus backing.

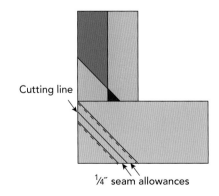

Cutting line

¼" seam allowances

SEWING BONUS BACKINGS

Step One

Draw the bonus pencil line ½" from the original pencil line on Unit 2. Place Unit 2 on top of Unit 1, right sides together, and stitch next to each pencil line.

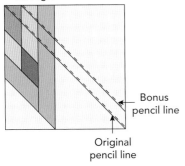

Wrong side of Unit 2

Bonus pencil line

Original pencil line

Step Two

Cut between the 2 stitching lines. Each unit will have a ¼" seam allowance.

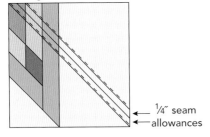

Cutting line

¼" seam allowances

SQUARING UP THE BONUS UNITS

I squared up all the bonus cut-offs before sewing them into wallhangings and backings. You will have small, medium, and very large cut-offs. I used the small and medium cut-offs to make great wallhangings, and the large cut-offs can be used for part of the backing.

Below are the measurements I used to square up the different units from the 30¾" square Stars. Of course, these measurements will be different when squaring up the bonus units from the lap-, queen-, and king-size Stars. Use a square ruler and make sure the "inner" triangle or "inner" square is squared up to the same size throughout. This is very important. If you don't, the seams won't butt together when you sew them into units and rows.

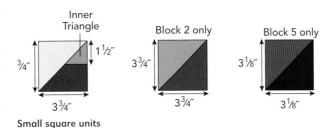

Small square units

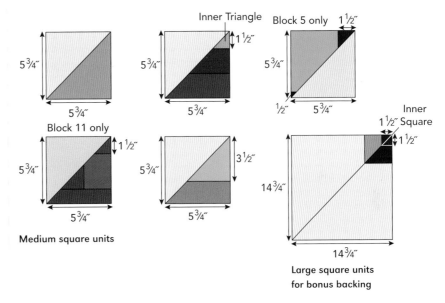

Medium square units

Large square units for bonus backing

INCREASING THE SIZE OF THE BONUS BACKING FOR THE WALLHANGING

To increase the bonus backing, simply add one border to the side and one border to the top of this unit. This will offset the bonus cut-off unit and keep the seam allowances on the Star wallhanging from aligning with the seam allowances of the backing. This prevents too much bulk in those areas, which would make it hard to quilt.

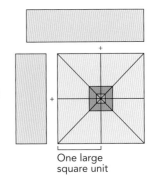

One large square unit

bonus wallhangings
and backings

On the following pages are the wallhangings and backings I made using the bonus cut-offs from each of the 14 wallhanging-size Stars. To make it quick and easy, I've included what size to square up the different units on each wallhanging diagram. If you choose to square up to a different size, just make sure you have the inner triangle or square the same size throughout the wallhanging, as described in Squaring Up the Bonus Units on page 59.

storm's eye

block 1 cut-offs

STORM'S EYE

- Size: 32$\frac{1}{2}$″ × 32$\frac{1}{2}$″

- 16 cut-offs from block 1

- Borders: Cut 6″ wide.

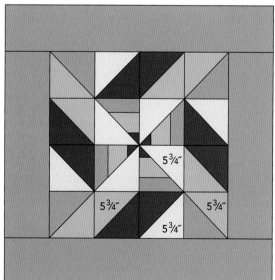

5$\frac{3}{4}$″

5$\frac{3}{4}$″   5$\frac{3}{4}$″

5$\frac{3}{4}$″

Block 1

Bonus backing

PINWHEEL CROSSING

▦ Size: 32½″ × 32½″

▦ 16 cut-offs from block 2

▦ A: Cut 2 pieces 2½″ × 11″.

▦ B: Cut 4 pieces 2½″ × 3¾″.

▦ Border: Cut 6″ wide.

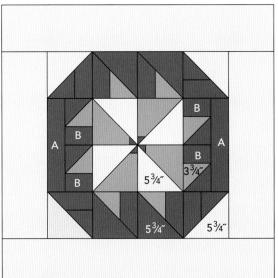

Block 2

Bonus backing

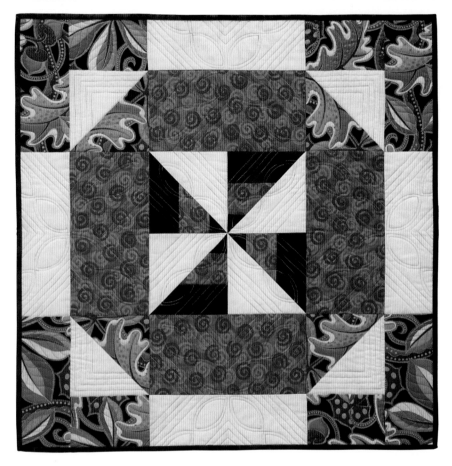

PINWHEEL PIZZAZZ

- Size: 28″ × 28″
- 8 cut-offs from block 3
- A: Cut 4 pieces 3¾″ × 11″.
- B: Cut 4 pieces 5¾″ × 11″.
- C: Cut 4 pieces 3¾″ × 5¾″.
- D: Cut 4 pieces 3¾″ × 9″.

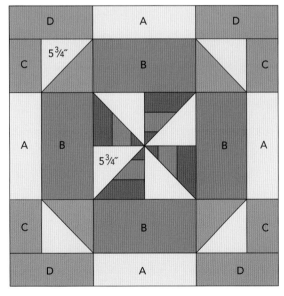

Block 3

Bonus backing

FLYING ARROWS

- Size: 24″ × 28″

- 16 cut-offs from block 4

- A: Cut 2 pieces $1\frac{3}{4}″ \times 21\frac{1}{2}″$.

- B: Cut 2 pieces $5\frac{3}{4}″ \times 21\frac{1}{2}″$.

- C: Cut 2 pieces $3\frac{3}{4}″ \times 11″$.

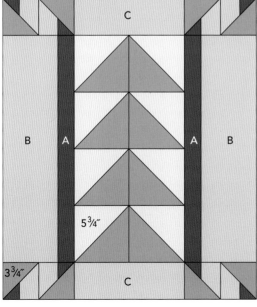

Block 4

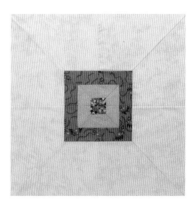

Bonus backing

SERENDIPITY STAR

- Size: $31^1/2'' \times 31^1/2''$
- 16 cut-offs from block 5
- A: Cut 4 pieces $5^3/4'' \times 5^3/4''$.
- B: Cut 2 pieces $5^3/4'' \times 5^3/4''$.
- C: Cut 4 pieces $2'' \times 21^1/2''$.
- D: Cut 4 pieces $4'' \times 21^1/2''$.
- E: Cut 4 pieces $5^1/2'' \times 5^1/2''$.

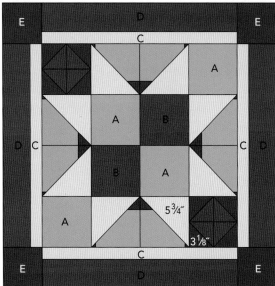

Block 5

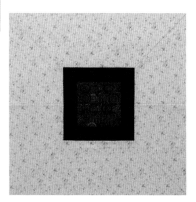

Bonus backing

sew simple

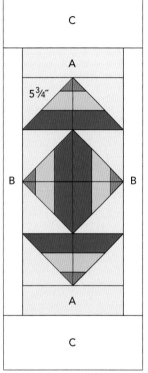

SEW SIMPLE

Size: 15″ × 38½″

8 cut-offs from block 6

A: Cut 2 pieces 3½″ × 11″.

B: Cut 2 pieces 2½″ × 27½″.

C: Cut 2 pieces 6″ × 15″.

Block 6

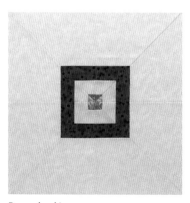

Bonus backing

FLIGHT OF FANCY

- Size: $26^{3}/_{4}'' \times 21^{1}/_{2}''$

- 8 cut-offs from block 7

- A: Cut 2 pieces $5^{3}/_{4}'' \times 5^{3}/_{4}''$.

- B: Cut 2 pieces $5^{3}/_{4}'' \times 11''$.

- C: Cut 2 pieces $5^{3}/_{4}'' \times 16^{1}/_{4}''$.

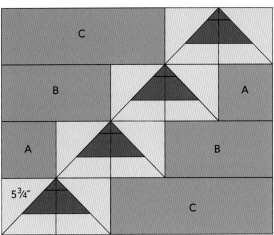

Block 7

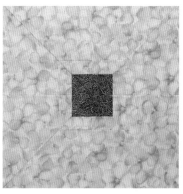

Bonus backing

hop, skip, or jump

HOP, SKIP, OR JUMP

Size: 29$\frac{1}{2}$″ × 29$\frac{1}{2}$″

12 cut-offs from block 8

A: Cut 4 pieces 5$\frac{3}{4}$″ × 5$\frac{3}{4}$″.

B: Cut 4 pieces 4$\frac{1}{2}$″ × 5$\frac{3}{4}$″.

C: Cut 16 pieces 2$\frac{1}{4}$″ × 4$\frac{1}{2}$″.

D: Cut 20 pieces 2$\frac{1}{4}$″ × 4$\frac{1}{2}$″.

E: Cut 4 pieces 4$\frac{1}{2}$″ × 4$\frac{1}{2}$″.

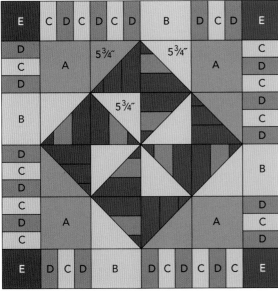

Block 8

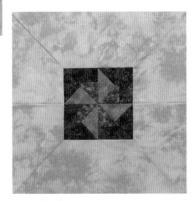

Bonus backing

PUZZLE IN A BOX

- Size: 30˝ × 30˝

- 12 cut-offs from block 9

- A: Cut 4 pieces 5¾˝ × 5¾˝.

- B: Cut 4 pieces 2˝ × 11˝.

- C: Cut 8 pieces 2 ˝ × 5¾˝.

- D: Cut 4 pieces 3¼˝ × 3¼˝.

- E: Cut 4 pieces 3¼˝ × 21½˝.

- F: Cut 4 pieces 2˝ × 2˝.

- G: Cut 8 pieces 2˝ × 3¼˝.

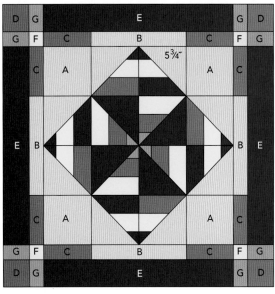

Block 9

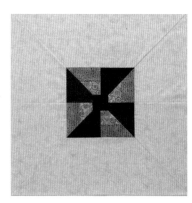

Bonus backing

partners

PARTNERS

- Size: $27^{1}/_{2}$″ × $27^{1}/_{2}$″

- 16 cut-offs from block 10

- A: Cut 8 pieces $2^{1}/_{2}$″ × 7″.

- B: Cut 8 pieces $2^{1}/_{2}$″ × $2^{1}/_{2}$″.

- Inner border: Cut 1″ wide.

- Outer border: Cut 3″ wide.

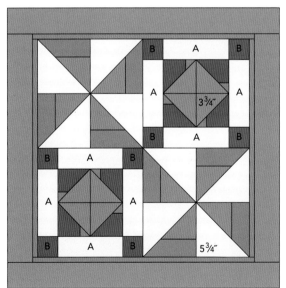

Block 10

Bonus backing

BALANCING ACT

- Size: 32″ × 26¾″

- 8 cut-offs from block 11

- A: Cut 8 pieces 5¾″ × 5¾″.

- B: Cut 8 pieces 5¾″ × 5¾″.

- C: Cut 6 circles 3½″ in diameter.

- D: Cut 6 pieces 5¾″ × 5¾″.

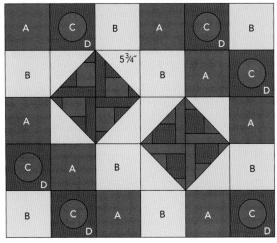

5¾″

Block 11

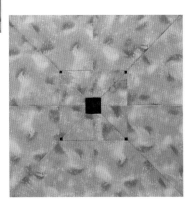

Bonus backing

fun and games

FUN AND GAMES

- Size: 32″ × 32″

- 8 cut-offs from block 12

- A: Cut 4 pieces $2\frac{5}{8}″ \times 11″$.

- B: Cut 4 pieces $2\frac{1}{2}″ \times 5\frac{3}{4}″$.

- C: Cut 4 pieces $2\frac{3}{8}″ \times 11″$.

- D: Cut 4 pieces $1\frac{3}{4}″ \times 11″$.

- E: Cut 4 pieces $1\frac{3}{4}″ \times 5\frac{3}{4}″$.

- F: Cut 4 pieces $2\frac{1}{2}″ \times 5\frac{3}{4}″$.

- G: Cut 8 pieces $2\frac{3}{8}″ \times 5\frac{3}{4}″$.

- H: Cut 8 pieces $3\frac{1}{8}″ \times 5\frac{3}{4}″$.

- I: Cut 8 pieces $2\frac{3}{8}″ \times 5\frac{3}{4}″$.

- J: Cut 8 pieces $3\frac{1}{8}″ \times 5\frac{3}{4}″$.

- K: Cut 4 pieces $1\frac{1}{4}″ \times 21\frac{1}{2}″$.

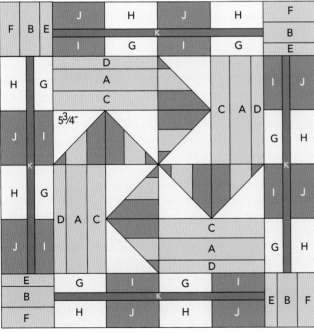

Block 12

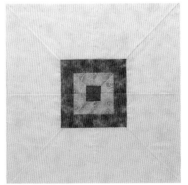

Bonus backing

NUTS AND BOLTS

- Size: 26½″ × 26½″

- 16 cut-offs from block 13

- A: Cut 2 pieces 2½″ × 7″.

- B: Cut 2 pieces 2½″ × 11″.

- C: Cut 4 pieces 2½″ × 3¾″.

- D: Cut 4 pieces 2½″ × 5¾″.

- Border: Cut 3″ wide.

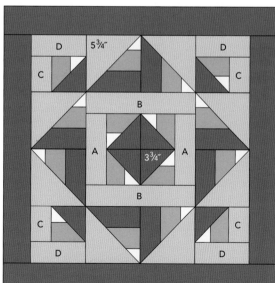

Block 13

Bonus backing

reflection

REFLECTION

- Size: $27\frac{1}{2}'' \times 27\frac{1}{2}''$

- 12 cut-offs from block 14

- A: Cut 4 pieces $5\frac{3}{4}'' \times 5\frac{3}{4}''$.

- B: Cut 4 pieces $2\frac{1}{2}'' \times 7''$.

- C: Cut 8 pieces $1'' \times 9\frac{1}{2}''$.

- D: Cut 4 pieces $2\frac{1}{2}'' \times 2\frac{1}{2}''$.

- E: Cut 16 pieces $1\frac{3}{4}'' \times 9\frac{1}{2}''$.

- F: Cut 8 pieces $3\frac{1}{2}'' \times 3\frac{1}{2}''$.

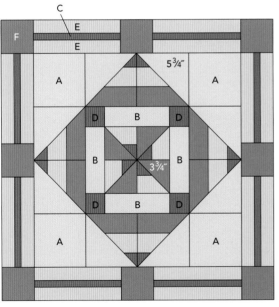

Block 14

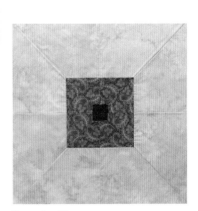

Bonus backing

quilt maps

 ## blazing lone star

SIZE: 42¾″ × 42¾″

MADE BY NANCY JOHNSON-SREBRO,
QUILTED BY VERONICA NURMI

Brighten any room or wall with this easy design. Make just one Star block, add borders, and you're done! I used Block 6, the classic Lone Star, for this wallhanging.

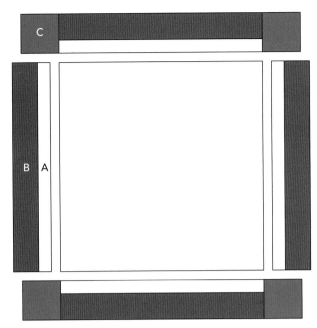

Wallhanging quilt map

30³⁄₄″ finished Star

Complete diagram

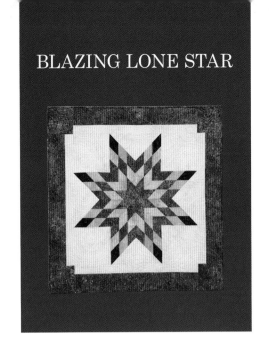

BLAZING LONE STAR

YARDAGE

Item	Color	Quantity Needed
* Inner Border (A)	☐	3/8 yard
* Outer Border (B)	◼	5/8 yard
Cornerstones (C)	◼	1/4 yard
Binding		1/2 yard
* Backing (D, E)		1 3/8 yards

*Based on cutting crosswise grain of the fabric. Backing yardage is based on using part of the bonus cut-offs.

CUTTING

Item	Color	# To Cut	Size
A	☐	4	2½" × 31¼"
B	◼	4	4¼" × 31¼"
C	◼	4	6¼" × 6¼"
D	Backing	1	19" × 46½"
E	Backing	1	19" × 28"

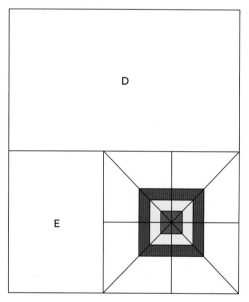

Backing; square up pieced bonus section to 28" × 28".

Bonus tablerunner; see page 65 for additional details.

joker's wild

SIZE: 68″ × 68″

MADE BY NANCY JOHNSON-SREBRO,
QUILTED BY VERONICA NURMI

I'm pretty tall and I've always had a problem with lap quilts not being long enough. I designed a lap quilt using Block 11 in a size that is long enough even for me! I call it a "luxury" lap quilt. Simply add wider borders on the top and bottom and then you'd have a twin-size quilt.

JOKER'S WILD

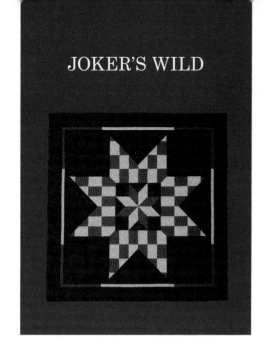

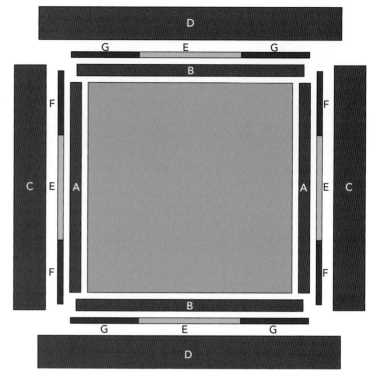

Luxury lap quilt map

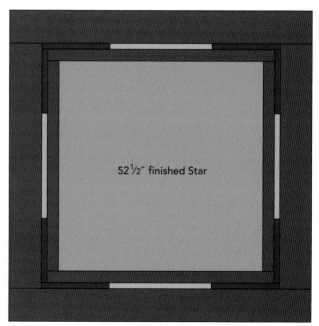

52$\frac{1}{2}$˝ finished Star

Complete diagram

YARDAGE

Item	Color	Quantity Needed
* Inner Border (A, B) * Outer Border (C, D)	■	2 yards
Middle Border (E)	▨	¼ yard
Middle Border (F, G)	■	¼ yard
Binding		¾ yard
* Backing (H, I)		3 yards

Based on cutting lengthwise grain of the fabric. Backing yardage is based on using part of the bonus cut-offs.

CUTTING

Item	Color	# To Cut	Size
A	■	2	2½" × 53"
B	■	2	2½" × 57"
C	■	2	5" × 59"
D	■	2	5" × 68"
E	▨	4	1½" × 28"
F	■	4	1½" × 15"
G	■	4	1½" × 16"
H	Backing	2	25" × 49½"
I	Backing	4	12¾" × 25"

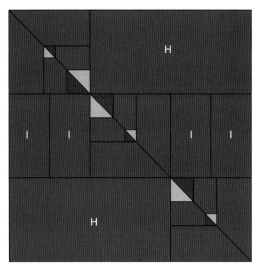

Backing; square up each pieced bonus section to 25˝ × 25˝.
You will have one cut-off left over.

rose garden

SIZE: 94″ × 94″

MADE BY NANCY JOHNSON-SREBRO,
QUILTED BY VERONICA NURMI

Gorgeous floral fabrics in soft colors make a lovely queen-size quilt. I used Block 12, but any of the blocks would make an equally stunning bed quilt—fit for a queen indeed.

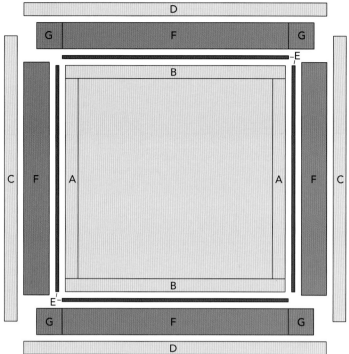

Queen quilt map

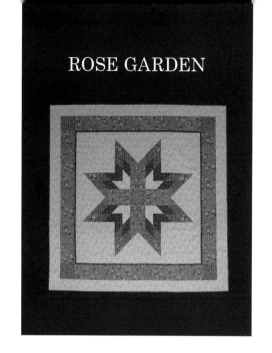

ROSE GARDEN

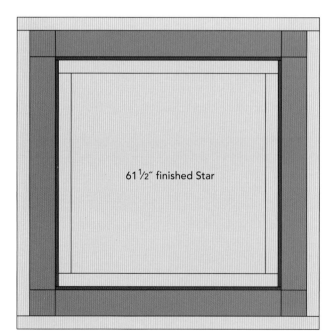

61½″ finished Star

Complete diagram

YARDAGE

Item	Color	Quantity Needed
* Inner Border (A, B) * Outer Border (C, D)		2¾ yards
Flat Piping (E)		½ yard
*Second Border (F)		2⅛ yards
Cornerstone (G)		⅜ yard
* Backing (H)		6 yards
Binding		1 yard

Based on cutting lengthwise grain of the fabric. Backing yardage is based on using part of the bonus cut-offs.

CUTTING

Item	Color	# To Cut	Size
A		2	4½″ × 62″
B		2	4½″ × 70″
C		2	4½″ × 86″
D		2	4½″ × 94″
E		8	1½″ × 40″
F		4	8½″ × 70″
G		4	8½″ × 8½″
H	Backing	2	40″ × 100½″

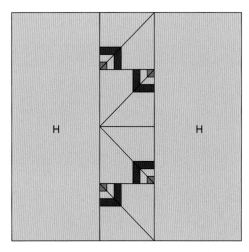

Backing; square up each pieced bonus section to 25½″ × 25½″.

FLAT PIPING INSTRUCTIONS

The piping strips are cut 1½″ wide and finish to ½″. Sew the short ends of the strips together. Press the strips in half lengthwise with wrong sides together. Trim these strips to the length and width of the quilt and follow the sewing diagrams.

Folded edge

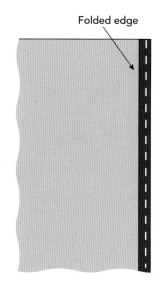

Align raw edges of piping with sides of quilt. Stitch, using very scant ¼″ seam.

Folded edge

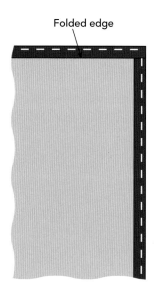

Align raw edges of piping with top/bottom edges of quilt. Stitch.

all-time favorite

SIZE: 107³/₄″ × 107³/₄″

MADE BY NANCY JOHNSON-SREBRO,
QUILTED BY VERONICA NURMI

Who would ever think one block could make a king-size quilt? Here's the timeless Lone Star, Block 6, in a simple but very effective setting. The print border and corner squares allow you to feature a fabric that you simply love or one that coordinates with your bedroom decor.

ALL-TIME FAVORITE

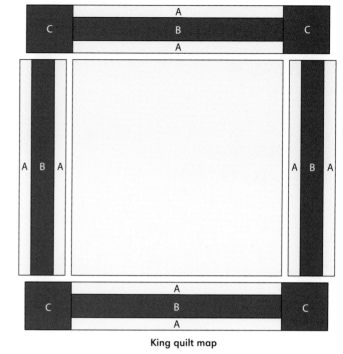

King quilt map

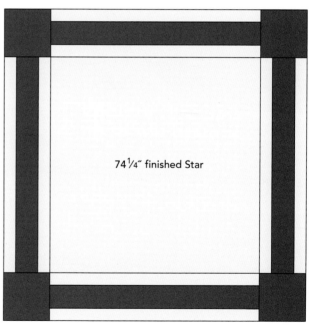

74$\frac{1}{4}$″ finished Star

Complete diagram

YARDAGE

Item	Color	Quantity Needed
* Inner and Outer Border (A)	☐	2¼ yards
* Middle Border (B) Cornerstone (C)	■	3¼ yards
* Backing (D)		6¾ yards
Binding		1 yard

Based on cutting lengthwise grain of the fabric. Backing yardage is based on using part of the bonus cut-offs.

CUTTING

Item	Color	# To Cut	Size
A	☐	8	4¾″ × 74¾″
B	■	4	8½″ × 74¾″
C	■	4	17″ × 17″
D	Backing	2	40″ × 116″

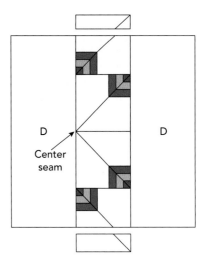

Backing; square up each pieced bonus section to 35½″ × 35½″. Match center of D to center seam of bonus strip. Stitch and trim excess top and bottom pieces.

Pretty in Pink and Brown by Ellen Pahl, 46″ × 46″.

Most of the quilts that I make are very scrappy. Why use just one fabric when you can use lots? I used a different light floral fabric for each of the center pieces of Block 7 and chose two different pink prints for the star points. I love this block—it reminds me of a snowflake.

Black Stars by Heidi Hopkinson Escobar,
machine quilted by Marion E. Lutz, $100\frac{1}{2}$″ × $100\frac{1}{2}$″.

As I planned this quilt, I decided to experiment with the
positive and negative space in Block 1 by using the background fabric for one section of the star points. I like the
twisty secondary black stars in the center of each block.
The large, gentle curves in the border were very easy to
piece. The quilting design was inspired by the designs of
Nan Moore (*The Best Blocks*) and Darlene Epp (*Pocket
Guide to Freehanding Meanderings*).

I Want to Be a Cowboy by **Wendy Hopkinson**,
machine quilted by **Marion E. Lutz**, 63″ × 88½″.

This quilt, using Block 5, reminds me of Saturday mornings
spent watching the "Singing Cowboy" on our black-and-
white TV. I just loved the print cowboy fabric and I hope this
quilt will be fun and comforting for future grandchildren. A
second quilt with cowgirl faces is in the works.

Winter Star **by Pamela Jones Quentin,
machine quilted by Patricia Prevallet, 71″ × 71″.**

I chose holiday colors for this queen-size Star quilt featuring
Block 2. Using the cream floral print enhances the traditional
red and green; the light print also highlights the red arms of
the star. A red border provides a great background for the
5″ prairie points.

Sweetheart Star by Laura Reidenbach, 35$\frac{1}{2}$″ × 44″.

As the mother of three sons, I was thrilled to learn that I was going to have a granddaughter. Little Reese Elizabeth was the inspiration for this baby quilt made of one Block 4 in pastel colors. Little "sweethearts" appear in the top and bottom borders. Because it was for a very special little sweetheart, I hand quilted it.

Grandma's Stars by Beth Anne Lowrie,
machine quilted by Candace Campbell, $82\frac{3}{4}" \times 82\frac{3}{4}"$.

I've always loved Star blocks. I chose Block 14, and in my quilt I wanted to honor the "stars" in our family. The four corner stars (from Nancy's earlier book, *Stars by Magic*) represent our four grandchildren, Ryan, Mikayla, Austin, and Makenzie. This quilt looks more complicated than it is due to the border fabric. It is a print fabric that looks pieced but isn't.

Garden Stars by Janet McCarroll, 62$\frac{1}{2}$″ × 74$\frac{3}{4}$″.

Every flower gardener knows that each year a certain
flower decides to show off and be the star of the garden.
The flower that outperforms all the others may be different
every year. This quilt represents my "garden stars." Block 10
is at center stage, while half of Block 5 peaks up from
below. The smallest star is a block from *Stars by Magic*.

Star of Hope by Molly Culp, 81″ × 81″.

I fell in love with the fabric in the center of Star Block 6. I used it as the focus fabric and chose fabrics in complementary colors and in various scales and designs. I used some blocks from Nancy's *Stars by Magic* book in the border. Sharon Schamber was kind enough to design the quilting patterns I used to quilt on my Gammill longarm quilting machine.

Daniel's Star Quilt by Debbie Donowski,
machine quilted by Val Hill, 96″ × 98″.

My son Daniel selected Block 9 and then chose the fabrics
he wanted for the star. I added three simple borders, in
coordinating colors, to finish the quilt's design.

resources

American & Efird, Inc.
Consumer Division
(Mettler Thread)
P.O. Box 507
Mt. Holly, NC 28120
www.amefird.com

Bear Country Quilting
1517 Deetz Road
Mt. Shasta, CA 96067
veronica.nurmi@gmail.com

Bernina of America, Inc.
3702 Prairie Lake Court
Aurora, IL 60504
www.berninausa.com

Fairfield Processing Corp.
www.poly-fil.com
(800) 980-8000

FreeSpirit
3430 Toringdon Way, Suite 301
Charlotte, NC 28277
www.freespiritfabric.com

Hobbs Bonded Fibers
P.O. Box 2521
Waco, TX 76702
www.hobbsbondedfibers.com

P&B Textiles
1580 Gilbreth Road
Burlingame, CA 94010
www.pbtex.com

Prym Consumer USA, Inc.
Spartanburg, SC 29304
www.dritz.com
www.omnigrid.com

RJR Fabrics
2203 Dominguez Street
Torrance, CA 90501
www.rjrfabrics.com

Robert Kaufman Fabrics
129 W. 132nd Street
Los Angeles, CA 90061
www.robertkaufman.com

Superior Threads
87 East 2580 South
St. George, UT 84790
www.superiorthreads.com

The Warm Company
5529 186th Place SW
Lynnwood, WA 98037
www.warmcompany.com

For more information,
ask for a free catalog:
C&T Publishing
P.O. Box 1456
Lafayette, CA 94549
(800) 284-1114
ctinfo@ctpub.com
www.ctpub.com

For quilting supplies:
Cotton Patch
1025 Brown Avenue
Lafayette, CA 94549
(800) 835-4418 or
(925) 283-7883
CottonPa@aol.com
www.quiltusa.com

about the author

Grandma Garrison was Nancy's mentor while she made her first quilt in 1972. Gram asked her to cut a 6-inch square template from paper and pin it on some fabric. Using regular scissors, quite dull, Nancy cut around the paper template. After cutting about two dozen squares, she noticed some of the squares were not the same size. Nancy called Gram and said, "My blocks don't seem to be the same size." Gram replied, "Are you cutting any of the paper template off when you cut around it?" Nancy replied, "No, only once in a while!" That was Nancy's first lesson in accuracy and it has stuck with her all these years. Today her hallmark is accuracy, and she stresses it with students and attributes the wide recognition of her work to its continued emphasis.

She has written several best-selling books, including *Featherweight 221: The Perfect Portable* and *Rotary Magic.* Nancy also refined how to work with squares and rectangles in her other best-selling books *Block Magic; Block Magic, Too!;* and *Stars by Magic.*

Recently she was granted a U.S. patent for her innovative technique used for making Eight-Point Stars from squares and rectangles.

Nancy has been a spokesperson and consultant for Omnigrid, a division of Prym Consumer USA, Inc., for more than eighteen years.

Her hobbies include reading mysteries, traveling to see children and grand-children, working in her flower gardens (they keep expanding), and making baby quilts for charity. In recent years she has donated more than 600 quilts to brighten the lives of needy children and parents. Nancy lives in Pennsylvania with her husband, Frank.

Great Titles

from  C&T PUBLISHING

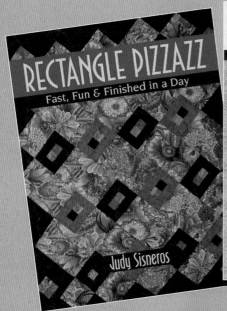

RECTANGLE PIZZAZZ
Fast, Fun & Finished in a Day
Judy Sisneros

Machine Quilting Solutions
TECHNIQUES FOR FAST & SIMPLE TO AWARD-WINNING DESIGNS
Christine Maraccini

fun with one block quilts
12 Projects in Multiple Sizes from 1 Simple Block
CHERYL MALKOWSKI

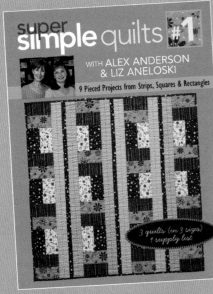

super simple quilts #1
WITH ALEX ANDERSON & LIZ ANELOSKI
9 Pieced Projects from Strips, Squares & Rectangles
3 quilts (in 3 sizes) 1 supply list

Easy & Elegant LONE STAR QUILTS
All the WOW Without the Work!
SHIRLEY STUTZ

Radiant Sunshine & Shadow
23 QUILTS WITH NINE-PATCH SPARKLE
Frost
erine Skow

placeholder